The Complete
Low Carb Diet Cookbook UK

1500 Days of Easy and Tasty Recipes to Master the Art of Low Carb Cooking | Full Color Edition

Kimberly T. Frank

Editor: LYN
Cover Art: ABR
Interior Design: FAIZAN
Food stylist: JO

Table Of Contents

Introduction

Welcome to a culinary adventure that will not only tantalize your taste buds but also revolutionize the way you approach nutrition and well-being. As you hold this *Low Carb Diet Cookbook* in your hands, you are embarking on a journey that celebrates the art of cooking while prioritizing your health and vitality. Within these pages, you will discover a treasure trove of delicious, nutritious, and low-carb recipes that will nourish your body and empower you to achieve your wellness goals.

In an age where fast-paced lifestyles and processed foods have become the norm, health concerns and obesity rates have reached alarming levels. As a society, we have drifted away from our roots, where natural and wholesome foods were the cornerstone of our diets. But fear not, for this cookbook aims to bring us back to the basics, reviving the timeless wisdom of consuming real, unprocessed ingredients while embracing the low-carb approach to eating.

The low-carb diet has emerged as a powerful ally in the quest for improved health and weight management. By reducing the intake of carbohydrates, which are often found in refined sugars, grains, and starchy foods, this dietary approach encourages the body to tap into its fat stores for energy. As a result, people often experience weight loss, increased energy levels, and better blood sugar control. Moreover, the low-carb lifestyle has shown promise in reducing the risk of various chronic diseases and promoting overall well-being.

Within these pages, you will encounter a diverse array of recipes that cater to all palates and occasions. From delectable breakfast options to hearty main courses and delectable desserts, each dish is thoughtfully crafted to strike the perfect balance between flavor and nutritional value. Drawing inspiration from cuisines around the world, these recipes prove that low-carb eating need not be dull or monotonous; instead, it can be a journey of culinary exploration and creativity.

In our pursuit of healthy living, it is essential to understand that nourishment is not merely about consuming food; it is about savoring each bite, appreciating the ingredients, and developing a mindful connection with what we eat. This cookbook seeks to instill in you a love for cooking and the empowerment that comes from taking charge of your health through the food choices you make.

Before you dive into the world of low-carb cooking, let us also address a common misconception: low-carb does not mean no-carb. Our bodies require carbohydrates, especially from non-starchy vegetables and some fruits, to function optimally. What sets this diet apart is its emphasis on making smart choices, opting for nutrient-dense, whole foods over processed, sugary alternatives. It is a celebration of the abundance nature provides while discarding the unnecessary additives and artificial flavors that often dominate modern diets.

As you embark on your low-carb journey, we encourage you to personalize your experience. Explore the flavors you love, experiment with new ingredients, and adapt these recipes to suit your preferences. Our goal is not to impose rigid rules but to inspire a sustainable lifestyle that you can embrace with joy and enthusiasm.

We are incredibly grateful to have you on this path with us, and we hope that the *Low Carb Diet Cookbook* becomes your trusted companion in the kitchen, supporting your efforts to lead a healthier and more fulfilling life. So, let the journey begin! May your culinary adventures be filled with joy, wellness, and the pure pleasure of eating delicious food that loves you back.

Chapter 1

Basics of the Low Carb Diet

Low-Carb, Not No-Carb

In the realm of dietary trends and weight loss strategies, the low-carb diet has garnered significant attention for its potential health benefits. However, it is often misconstrued as a diet that entirely eliminates carbohydrates from the menu. To dispel this misconception and gain a better understanding of the low-carb approach, we must recognize that it's about finding a balance in our carbohydrate consumption rather than eliminating them altogether.

THE LOW-CARB PHILOSOPHY

At its core, the low-carb diet emphasizes reducing the intake of carbohydrates, particularly those derived from refined sugars and highly processed foods. Carbohydrates are one of the three essential macronutrients, alongside proteins and fats, and they play a vital role in providing energy to our bodies. However, in the modern diet, excessive consumption of refined carbohydrates has been linked to various health issues, including obesity, type 2 diabetes, and cardiovascular diseases.

The low-carb philosophy revolves around opting for healthier, nutrient-dense carbohydrate sources while minimizing the intake of empty, high-calorie carbs that lack nutritional value. By doing so, the body is encouraged to enter a state of ketosis, where it relies on fat stores for fuel rather than carbohydrates, leading to potential weight loss and improved metabolic health.

THE ROLE OF CARBOHYDRATES

Carbohydrates come in various forms, including simple sugars and complex carbohydrates. Simple sugars, found in sugary snacks, candies, and beverages, provide quick energy but lack essential nutrients. They lead to rapid spikes in blood sugar levels, which can result in energy crashes and increased hunger, prompting overeating.

On the other hand, complex carbohydrates, present in whole grains, legumes, vegetables, and fruits, are a more sustainable energy source. They contain fiber, vitamins, and minerals, offering greater satiety and supporting overall health. These are the types of carbohydrates that should form the foundation of a balanced low-carb diet.

CARBOHYDRATES IN THE LOW-CARB DIET

The low-carb diet encourages individuals to choose their carbohydrate sources wisely. While it advocates a significant reduction in refined carbohydrates like white bread, pasta, and sugary treats, it allows for a moderate intake of nutrient-rich carbs that provide essential nutrients and contribute to overall well-being.

NON-STARCHY VEGETABLES

Non-starchy vegetables are low in carbohydrates and high in fiber, making them an excellent choice for a low-carb diet. Leafy greens, broccoli, cauliflower, zucchini, and bell peppers are examples of nutritious vegetables that should feature prominently in low-carb meals.

BERRIES

Berries, such as blueberries, strawberries, and raspberries, are lower in sugar compared to other fruits and can be enjoyed in moderation as part of a low-carb diet. They are rich in antioxidants and provide essential vitamins and minerals.

NUTS AND SEEDS

Nuts and seeds are a source of healthy fats, protein, and fiber. While they contain some carbohydrates, they offer a satisfying crunch and a wealth of nutrients.

LEGUMES

Legumes, including lentils, chickpeas, and black beans, are an excellent plant-based protein source with a moderate amount of carbohydrates. When consumed in appropriate portions, they can be included in a balanced low-carb diet.

GRAINS

Whole grains like quinoa, oats, and barley are higher in fiber and nutrients compared to refined grains. They can be consumed in moderation for those who prefer to include some grains in their low-carb lifestyle.

THE IMPORTANCE OF MODERATION

A critical aspect of the low-carb approach is moderation. While the diet emphasizes reducing carbohydrates, it does not entail eliminating them entirely. Completely cutting out an entire food group can lead to nutritional imbalances and potential deficiencies. Instead, it is essential to strike a balance that suits individual needs and health goals.

For some individuals, a very low-carb or

ketogenic diet may be beneficial for specific health conditions or weight loss objectives. However, for others, a moderately low-carb approach that includes nutrient-dense carbohydrates can be equally effective in achieving health and wellness goals.

Benefits of Low-Carb Diets

Low-carb diets have emerged as a popular and effective approach to improving health and achieving various wellness goals. These dietary regimens advocate reducing carbohydrate intake while emphasizing protein, healthy fats, and nutrient-dense foods. While individual results may vary, numerous studies and real-life experiences attest to the many benefits that low-carb diets can offer. Let's explore some of the key advantages of adopting a low-carb lifestyle:

WEIGHT LOSS AND SATIETY

One of the most significant benefits of low-carb diets is their ability to promote weight loss and long-term weight management. By reducing carbohydrate intake, the body shifts its primary fuel source from carbohydrates to stored fat. This metabolic shift leads to the production of ketones, which are molecules produced when fat is broken down. As a result, the body becomes more efficient at burning fat for energy, ultimately aiding in weight loss.

Moreover, low-carb diets often increase feelings of fullness and satiety due to the higher consumption of protein and healthy fats. This can lead to reduced overall calorie intake and fewer cravings for sugary and processed foods, making it easier to maintain a calorie deficit necessary for weight loss.

IMPROVED BLOOD SUGAR CONTROL

For individuals with type 2 diabetes or insulin resistance, low-carb diets can be particularly beneficial. Carbohydrates are broken down into glucose (sugar) in the body, leading to an increase in blood sugar levels. By reducing carbohydrate intake, the fluctuations in blood sugar levels are minimized, helping individuals better manage their condition and potentially reduce the need for diabetes medications.

ENHANCED CARDIOVASCULAR HEALTH

Low-carb diets have been associated with improvements in several risk factors for cardiovascular disease. They often lead to reductions in triglycerides, which are fats in the blood associated with an increased risk of heart disease. Additionally, low-carb diets can raise levels of high-density lipoprotein (HDL) cholesterol, often referred to as "good" cholesterol, which plays a protective role in heart health.

Furthermore, low-carb diets may help decrease blood pressure levels, which are crucial for maintaining cardiovascular well-being and reducing the risk of hypertension-related complications.

BETTER MANAGEMENT OF METABOLIC SYNDROME

Metabolic syndrome is a cluster of conditions, including abdominal obesity, high blood pressure, high blood sugar levels, and abnormal lipid levels, which collectively increase the risk of heart disease, stroke, and type 2 diabetes. Low-carb diets have been shown to be effective in addressing many of these factors, making them a potential therapeutic approach for managing metabolic syndrome.

ENHANCED MENTAL CLARITY AND ENERGY LEVELS

Some individuals report improved mental clarity and sustained energy levels when following a low-carb diet. The steady release of energy from fats may help prevent energy crashes commonly associated with high-carbohydrate meals.

APPETITE CONTROL AND REDUCED CRAVINGS

By reducing the consumption of refined carbohydrates and sugar, low-carb diets can help stabilize blood sugar levels, resulting in fewer hunger pangs and reduced cravings. This can make it easier to adhere

to the dietary plan and make healthier food choices over the long term.

Potentially Lower Risk of Chronic Diseases

Several observational studies have suggested that low-carb diets may be associated with a reduced risk of certain chronic diseases, such as certain types of cancer and neurodegenerative conditions. However, more research is needed to establish definitive causal relationships.

It's essential to note that while low-carb diets offer numerous benefits, they may not be suitable for everyone. Pregnant or breastfeeding women, athletes, and individuals with certain medical conditions should consult with a healthcare professional before making significant dietary changes. Additionally, the long-term sustainability and individual response to low-carb diets may vary, so finding an approach that aligns with personal preferences and health goals is crucial.

Tips for Success

EDUCATE YOURSELF

Take the time to learn about the principles and guidelines of a low-carb diet. Understand which foods are high in carbohydrates and which ones are suitable for a low-carb lifestyle.

PLAN YOUR MEALS

Plan your meals ahead of time to ensure you have nutritious and low-carb options readily available. This will help you avoid making impulsive food choices when hungry.

FOCUS ON WHOLE FOODS

Prioritize whole, unprocessed foods such as vegetables, fruits (in moderation), lean proteins, healthy fats, and nuts. These foods are rich in nutrients and will keep you feeling satisfied.

READ LABELS

Be mindful of food labels, as many processed foods may contain hidden sugars and high carb content. Avoid products with added sugars and opt for whole-food alternatives.

STAY HYDRATED

Drink plenty of water throughout the day. Sometimes, feelings of hunger can be mistaken for thirst, and staying hydrated can help curb unnecessary snacking.

PLAN FOR SNACKS

Have low-carb snacks readily available, such as nuts, cheese, and vegetables with hummus, to prevent reaching for high-carb options when hunger strikes between meals.

MONITOR PORTION SIZES

While low-carb foods are generally more satiating, portion control is still essential. Be mindful of portion sizes to avoid overeating.

BE MINDFUL OF HIDDEN CARBS

Some seemingly healthy foods, like certain fruits and vegetables, can still contain significant carbs. Be mindful of their carb content and include them in moderation.

BE PREPARED FOR SOCIAL SITUATIONS

When dining out or attending social gatherings, plan ahead by researching menu options or bringing a low-carb dish to share.

INCLUDE HEALTHY FATS

Incorporate healthy fats such as avocados, olive oil, coconut oil, and nuts into your meals. These fats are essential for energy and satiety on a low-carb diet.

FIND LOW-CARB SUBSTITUTES

Look for low-carb substitutes for your favorite high-carb dishes. For example, cauliflower rice can replace regular rice, and zucchini noodles can be a great alternative to pasta.

BE PATIENT AND FLEXIBLE

Everyone's body responds differently to dietary changes. Be patient with yourself, and don't be afraid to adjust your approach if something isn't working for you.

TRACK YOUR PROGRESS

Consider keeping a food journal or using a mobile app to track your meals and progress. This can help you identify patterns, track your carb intake, and stay accountable.

SEEK SUPPORT

Joining a low-carb community or finding a diet buddy can provide motivation and support on your journey.

FOCUS ON LONG-TERM SUSTAINABILITY

Embrace the low-carb lifestyle as a long-term approach to health and well-being, rather than a short-term diet. Sustainable habits yield lasting results.

Chapter 2

28-Day Meal Plan

Week 1

Congratulations on taking the first step towards a healthier you! Embarking on a low carb diet can be challenging, but remember that you have the power to transform your eating habits and improve your well-being. Embrace this week as a fresh start, where you bid farewell to processed carbs and welcome wholesome alternatives. Focus on incorporating lean proteins, leafy greens, and healthy fats into your meals. It might be tough initially, but stay determined and remind yourself of the incredible benefits you will reap from this dietary shift. Your body will thank you, and the results will soon become evident.

Meal Plan	Breakfast	Snack	Lunch	Dinner	Snack
Day-1	Five Greens Smoothie	Cheesy Stuffed Jalapeños	Grilled Chicken Wings	Jerked Beef Stew	Cheesy Stuffed Jalapeños
	Calories:124 | Fat: 7.8g | Net Carbs: 2.9g | Protein: 3.2g	Calories: 189 | Fat: 13.2g | Carbs: 4.9g | Protein: 12.7g | Fiber: 1.1g	Calories:216 | Fat: 11.5g | Net Carbs: 4.3g | Protein: 18.5g	Calories:235 | Fat: 13.4g | Net Carbs:2.8g | Protein 25.8g	Calories: 189 | Fat: 13.2g | Carbs: 4.9g | Protein: 12.7g | Fiber: 1.1g
Day-2	Five Greens Smoothie	Cheesy Stuffed Jalapeños	Grilled Chicken Wings	Jerked Beef Stew	Cheesy Stuffed Jalapeños
	Calories:124 | Fat: 7.8g | Net Carbs: 2.9g | Protein: 3.2g	Calories: 189 | Fat: 13.2g | Carbs: 4.9g | Protein: 12.7g | Fiber: 1.1g	Calories:216 | Fat: 11.5g | Net Carbs: 4.3g | Protein: 18.5g	Calories:235 | Fat: 13.4g | Net Carbs:2.8g | Protein 25.8g	Calories: 189 | Fat: 13.2g | Carbs: 4.9g | Protein: 12.7g | Fiber: 1.1g
Day-3	Five Greens Smoothie	Cheesy Stuffed Jalapeños	Grilled Chicken Wings	Jerked Beef Stew	Cheesy Stuffed Jalapeños
	Calories:124 | Fat: 7.8g | Net Carbs: 2.9g | Protein: 3.2g	Calories: 189 | Fat: 13.2g | Carbs: 4.9g | Protein: 12.7g | Fiber: 1.1g	Calories:216 | Fat: 11.5g | Net Carbs: 4.3g | Protein: 18.5g	Calories:235 | Fat: 13.4g | Net Carbs:2.8g | Protein 25.8g	Calories: 189 | Fat: 13.2g | Carbs: 4.9g | Protein: 12.7g | Fiber: 1.1g
Day-4	Five Greens Smoothie	Cheesy Stuffed Jalapeños	Grilled Chicken Wings	Jerked Beef Stew	Cheesy Stuffed Jalapeños

		Calories:124 | Fat: 7.8g | Net Carbs: 2.9g | Protein: 3.2g	Calories: 189 | Fat: 13.2g | Carbs: 4.9g | Protein: 12.7g | Fiber: 1.1g	Calories:216 | Fat: 11.5g | Net Carbs: 4.3g | Protein: 18.5g	Calories:235 | Fat: 13.4g | Net Carbs:2.8g | Protein 25.8g	Calories: 189 | Fat: 13.2g | Carbs: 4.9g | Protein: 12.7g | Fiber: 1.1g
Day-5	Vegetable Keto Bread	Cheesy Stuffed Jalapeños	Thai-Style Tuna Fillets	Spicy Glazed Aubergine	Cheesy Stuffed Jalapeños
		Calories:283 | Fat: 17g | Net Carbs:3.5g | Protein 13g	Calories: 189 | Fat: 13.2g | Carbs: 4.9g | Protein: 12.7g | Fiber: 1.1g	Calories: 389 | Fat: 17.9g | Carbs: 3.5g | Protein: 50.3g | Fiber: 0.3g	Calories: 102 |Fat: 7g | Carbs: 8g | Protein: 1.6g | Fiber: 4.7g	Calories: 189 | Fat: 13.2g | Carbs: 4.9g | Protein: 12.7g | Fiber: 1.1g
Day-6	Vegetable Keto Bread	Coconut Ginger Macaroons	Thai-Style Tuna Fillets	Spicy Glazed Aubergine	Coconut Ginger Macaroons
		Calories:283 | Fat: 17g | Net Carbs:3.5g | Protein 13g	Calories:97 | Fat: 3.5g | Net Carbs: 0.3g | Protein: 6.8g	Calories: 389 | Fat: 17.9g | Carbs: 3.5g | Protein: 50.3g | Fiber: 0.3g	Calories: 102 |Fat: 7g | Carbs: 8g | Protein: 1.6g | Fiber: 4.7g	Calories:97 | Fat: 3.5g | Net Carbs: 0.3g | Protein: 6.8g
Day-7	Vegetable Keto Bread	Coconut Ginger Macaroons	Thai-Style Tuna Fillets	Spicy Glazed Aubergine	Coconut Ginger Macaroons
		Calories:283 | Fat: 17g | Net Carbs:3.5g | Protein 13g	Calories:97 | Fat: 3.5g | Net Carbs: 0.3g | Protein: 6.8g	Calories: 389 | Fat: 17.9g | Carbs: 3.5g | Protein: 50.3g | Fiber: 0.3g	Calories: 102 |Fat: 7g | Carbs: 8g | Protein: 1.6g | Fiber: 4.7g	Calories:97 | Fat: 3.5g | Net Carbs: 0.3g | Protein: 6.8g

Week 2

You've made it through the first week, and now it's time to build momentum. As you continue on your low carb journey, you'll likely notice some positive changes: increased energy, improved mental clarity, and even some weight loss. This week, let's take it up a notch. Experiment with new recipes that excite your taste buds while still adhering to the low carb principles. Seek inspiration from colorful vegetables, nourishing seafood, and vibrant spices. Remember, your commitment to this healthier lifestyle is forging a path towards long-term well-being. Stay focused, and keep pushing forward!

Meal Plan	Breakfast	Snack	Lunch	Dinner	Snack
Day-1	Egg in a Cheesy Spinach Nests	Easy Caprese Appetizer	Basil Turkey Meatballs	Greek Pork with Olives	Easy Caprese Appetizer
	Calories:230 | Fat: 17.5g | Net Carbs: 4g | Protein: 12g	Calories: 141 | Fat: 8.2g | Carbs: 3.3g | Protein: 12.9g | Fiber: 1g	Calories:310 | Fat: 26g | Net Carbs: 2g | Protein: 22g	Calories:415 | Fat: 25.2g | Net Carbs: 2.2g | Protein: 36g	Calories: 141 | Fat: 8.2g | Carbs: 3.3g | Protein: 12.9g | Fiber: 1g
Day-2	Egg in a Cheesy Spinach Nests	Easy Caprese Appetizer	Basil Turkey Meatballs	Greek Pork with Olives	Easy Caprese Appetizer
	Calories:230 | Fat: 17.5g | Net Carbs: 4g | Protein: 12g	Calories: 141 | Fat: 8.2g | Carbs: 3.3g | Protein: 12.9g | Fiber: 1g	Calories:310 | Fat: 26g | Net Carbs: 2g | Protein: 22g	Calories:415 | Fat: 25.2g | Net Carbs: 2.2g | Protein: 36g	Calories: 141 | Fat: 8.2g | Carbs: 3.3g | Protein: 12.9g | Fiber: 1g
Day-3	Egg in a Cheesy Spinach Nests	Easy Caprese Appetizer	Basil Turkey Meatballs	Greek Pork with Olives	Easy Caprese Appetizer
	Calories:230 | Fat: 17.5g | Net Carbs: 4g | Protein: 12g	Calories: 141 | Fat: 8.2g | Carbs: 3.3g | Protein: 12.9g | Fiber: 1g	Calories:310 | Fat: 26g | Net Carbs: 2g | Protein: 22g	Calories:415 | Fat: 25.2g | Net Carbs: 2.2g | Protein: 36g	Calories: 141 | Fat: 8.2g | Carbs: 3.3g | Protein: 12.9g | Fiber: 1g
Day-4	Egg in a Cheesy Spinach Nests	Easy Caprese Appetizer	Basil Turkey Meatballs	Greek Pork with Olives	Easy Caprese Appetizer
	Calories:230 | Fat: 17.5g | Net Carbs: 4g | Protein: 12g	Calories: 141 | Fat: 8.2g | Carbs: 3.3g | Protein: 12.9g | Fiber: 1g	Calories:310 | Fat: 26g | Net Carbs: 2g | Protein: 22g	Calories:415 | Fat: 25.2g | Net Carbs: 2.2g | Protein: 36g	Calories: 141 | Fat: 8.2g | Carbs: 3.3g | Protein: 12.9g | Fiber: 1g
Day-5	Bakery-Style Mini Muffins	Easy Caprese Appetizer	Summer Salad with Cod Fish	Parsnip and Carrot Fries with Aioli	Easy Caprese Appetizer
	Calories: 85| Fat: 6.4g | Carbs: 3.1g | Protein: 4.1g | Fiber: 0g	Calories: 141 | Fat: 8.2g | Carbs: 3.3g | Protein: 12.9g | Fiber: 1g	Calories: 276 | Fat: 6.9g | Carbs: 6.4g | Protein: 42.7g | Fiber: 1.7g	Calories:155 | Fat: 7.4g | Net Carbs: 7.4g | Protein: 2.1g	Calories: 141 | Fat: 8.2g | Carbs: 3.3g | Protein: 12.9g | Fiber: 1g

Day-6	Bakery-Style Mini Muffins	Lazy Strawberry Mini Cakes	Summer Salad with Cod Fish	Parsnip and Carrot Fries with Aioli	Lazy Strawberry Mini Cakes
	Calories: 85| Fat: 6.4g | Carbs: 3.1g | Protein: 4.1g | Fiber: 0g	Calories:311 | Fat: 28.3g | Net Carbs:6.4g | Protein 13.7g	Calories: 276 | Fat: 6.9g | Carbs: 6.4g | Protein: 42.7g | Fiber: 1.7g	Calories:155 | Fat: 7.4g | Net Carbs: 7.4g | Protein: 2.1g	Calories:311 | Fat: 28.3g | Net Carbs:6.4g | Protein 13.7g
Day-7	Bakery-Style Mini Muffins	Lazy Strawberry Mini Cakes	Summer Salad with Cod Fish	Parsnip and Carrot Fries with Aioli	Lazy Strawberry Mini Cakes
	Calories: 85| Fat: 6.4g | Carbs: 3.1g | Protein: 4.1g | Fiber: 0g	Calories:311 | Fat: 28.3g | Net Carbs:6.4g | Protein 13.7g	Calories: 276 | Fat: 6.9g | Carbs: 6.4g | Protein: 42.7g | Fiber: 1.7g	Calories:155 | Fat: 7.4g | Net Carbs: 7.4g | Protein: 2.1g	Calories:311 | Fat: 28.3g | Net Carbs:6.4g | Protein 13.7g

Week 3

You're doing amazing! By now, you've experienced the transformative power of a low carb diet, and it's time to take things to the next level. This week, let's fine-tune your meal plan and optimize your nutrient intake. Consider incorporating more plant-based proteins like tofu or lentils, along with a variety of nuts and seeds for added crunch and healthy fats. Explore the world of low carb snacks and find options that satisfy your cravings without derailing your progress. Trust the process, stay disciplined, and remind yourself that each day brings you closer to your health goals.

Meal Plan	Breakfast	Snack	Lunch	Dinner	Snack
Day-1	Bacon Tomato Cups	Coconut Cheesecake	Carolina Chicken Mull	Creamy Reuben Soup	Coconut Cheesecake
	Calories:425 | Fat: 45.2g | Net Carbs: 4.3g | Protein: 16.2g	Calories:256 | Fat: 25g | Net Carbs: 3g | Protein: 5g	Calories: 343 | Fat: 26.7g | Carbs: 3.8g | Protein: 20.9g | Fiber: 0.2g	Calories:450 | Net Carbs: 8g | Fat: 37g | Protein 23g	Calories:256 | Fat: 25g | Net Carbs: 3g | Protein: 5g
Day-2	Bacon Tomato Cups	Coconut Cheesecake	Carolina Chicken Mull	Creamy Reuben Soup	Coconut Cheesecake
	Calories:425 | Fat: 45.2g | Net Carbs: 4.3g | Protein: 16.2g	Calories:256 | Fat: 25g | Net Carbs: 3g | Protein: 5g	Calories: 343 | Fat: 26.7g | Carbs: 3.8g | Protein: 20.9g | Fiber: 0.2g	Calories:450 | Net Carbs: 8g | Fat: 37g | Protein 23g	Calories:256 | Fat: 25g | Net Carbs: 3g | Protein: 5g
Day-3	Bacon Tomato Cups	Coconut Cheesecake	Carolina Chicken Mull	Creamy Reuben Soup	Coconut Cheesecake
	Calories:425 | Fat: 45.2g | Net Carbs: 4.3g | Protein: 16.2g	Calories:256 | Fat: 25g | Net Carbs: 3g | Protein: 5g	Calories: 343 | Fat: 26.7g | Carbs: 3.8g | Protein: 20.9g | Fiber: 0.2g	Calories:450 | Net Carbs: 8g | Fat: 37g | Protein 23g	Calories:256 | Fat: 25g | Net Carbs: 3g | Protein: 5g
Day-4	Bacon Tomato Cups	Coconut Cheesecake	Carolina Chicken Mull	Creamy Reuben Soup	Coconut Cheesecake
	Calories:425 | Fat: 45.2g | Net Carbs: 4.3g | Protein: 16.2g	Calories:256 | Fat: 25g | Net Carbs: 3g | Protein: 5g	Calories: 343 | Fat: 26.7g | Carbs: 3.8g | Protein: 20.9g | Fiber: 0.2g	Calories:450 | Net Carbs: 8g | Fat: 37g | Protein 23g	Calories:256 | Fat: 25g | Net Carbs: 3g | Protein: 5g

Day-5	Bacon Tomato Cups	Coconut Cheesecake	Salmon Panzanella	Creamy Reuben Soup	Coconut Cheesecake
	Calories:425 | Fat: 45.2g | Net Carbs: 4.3g | Protein: 16.2g	Calories:256 | Fat: 25g | Net Carbs: 3g | Protein: 5g	Calories:338 | Fat: 21.7g | Net Carbs: 3.1g | Protein: 28.5g	Calories:450 | Net Carbs: 8g | Fat: 37g | Protein 23g	Calories:256 | Fat: 25g | Net Carbs: 3g | Protein: 5g
Day-6	Dark Chocolate Smoothie	Coconut Cheesecake	Salmon Panzanella	Creamy Reuben Soup	Coconut Cheesecake
	Calories:335 | Fat: 31.7g| Net Carbs: 12.7g | Protein: 7g	Calories:256 | Fat: 25g | Net Carbs: 3g | Protein: 5g	Calories:338 | Fat: 21.7g | Net Carbs: 3.1g | Protein: 28.5g	Calories:450 | Net Carbs: 8g | Fat: 37g | Protein 23g	Calories:256 | Fat: 25g | Net Carbs: 3g | Protein: 5g
Day-7	Dark Chocolate Smoothie	Raspberry Nut Truffles	Salmon Panzanella	Salmon Panzanella	Raspberry Nut Truffles
	Calories:335 | Fat: 31.7g| Net Carbs: 12.7g | Protein: 7g	Calories:251 | Fat: 18.3g | Net Carbs: 3.5g | Protein: 12g	Calories:338 | Fat: 21.7g | Net Carbs: 3.1g | Protein: 28.5g	Calories:338 | Fat: 21.7g | Net Carbs: 3.1g | Protein: 28.5g	Calories:251 | Fat: 18.3g | Net Carbs: 3.5g | Protein: 12g

Week 4

You've reached the final week of your low carb meal plan, and your dedication has paid off. Take a moment to reflect on how far you've come. Notice the increased vitality, improved digestion, and perhaps even a few inches shed from your waistline. As you approach the finish line, it's important to maintain your focus and continue making mindful choices. Plan your meals with intention, choosing whole foods that nourish your body and support your long-term well-being. Remember, this is not just a temporary diet but a lifestyle change. Embrace the empowerment that comes with knowing you have the ability to create lasting positive change in your life. You've got this!

Meal Plan	Breakfast	Snack	Lunch	Dinner	Snack
Day-1	Coconut Flour Bagels	Simple Nutty Crepes	Turkey Fajita Skillet	Veggie Chuck Roast Beef	Puffy Anise Cookies
	Calories:426 | Fat: 19.1g | Net Carbs: 0.4g | Protein: 33.1g	Calories: 260 | Fat: 21.7g | Carbs: 6.9g | Protein: 11.6g | Fiber: 3.8g	Calories: 212| Fat: 9.2g | Carbs: 5.6g | Protein: 26g | Fiber: 1.2g	Calories:325 | Fat: 17.8g | Net Carbs:5.6g | Protein 31.5g	Calories: 142 | Fat: 13g | Carbs: 5.2g | Protein: 3.5g | Fiber: 2.4g

Day-2	Coconut Flour Bagels	Simple Nutty Crepes	Turkey Fajita Skillet	Veggie Chuck Roast Beef	Puffy Anise Cookies
	Calories:426 | Fat: 19.1g | Net Carbs: 0.4g | Protein: 33.1g	Calories: 260 | Fat: 21.7g | Carbs: 6.9g | Protein: 11.6g | Fiber: 3.8g	Calories: 212| Fat: 9.2g | Carbs: 5.6g | Protein: 26g | Fiber: 1.2g	Calories:325 | Fat: 17.8g | Net Carbs:5.6g | Protein 31.5g	Calories: 142 | Fat: 13g | Carbs: 5.2g | Protein: 3.5g | Fiber: 2.4g
Day-3	Coconut Flour Bagels	Simple Nutty Crepes	Turkey Fajita Skillet	Veggie Chuck Roast Beef	Puffy Anise Cookies
	Calories:426 | Fat: 19.1g | Net Carbs: 0.4g | Protein: 33.1g	Calories: 260 | Fat: 21.7g | Carbs: 6.9g | Protein: 11.6g | Fiber: 3.8g	Calories: 212| Fat: 9.2g | Carbs: 5.6g | Protein: 26g | Fiber: 1.2g	Calories:325 | Fat: 17.8g | Net Carbs:5.6g | Protein 31.5g	Calories: 142 | Fat: 13g | Carbs: 5.2g | Protein: 3.5g | Fiber: 2.4g
Day-4	Coconut Flour Bagels	Simple Nutty Crepes	Turkey Fajita Skillet	Veggie Chuck Roast Beef	Puffy Anise Cookies
	Calories:426 | Fat: 19.1g | Net Carbs: 0.4g | Protein: 33.1g	Calories: 260 | Fat: 21.7g | Carbs: 6.9g | Protein: 11.6g | Fiber: 3.8g	Calories: 212| Fat: 9.2g | Carbs: 5.6g | Protein: 26g | Fiber: 1.2g	Calories:325 | Fat: 17.8g | Net Carbs:5.6g | Protein 31.5g	Calories: 142 | Fat: 13g | Carbs: 5.2g | Protein: 3.5g | Fiber: 2.4g
Day-5	Swiss-Style Italian Sausage	Simple Nutty Crepes	Sour Cream Salmon with Parmesan	German Fried Cabbage	Puffy Anise Cookies
	Calories:567 | Fat: 45g | Net Carbs: 7.6g | Protein: 34g	Calories: 260 | Fat: 21.7g | Carbs: 6.9g | Protein: 11.6g | Fiber: 3.8g	Calories:288 | Fat: 23.4g | Net Carbs: 1.2g | Protein: 16.2g	Calories: 243 | Fat: 22.2g | Carbs: 6.8g | Protein: 6.5g | Fiber: 1.9g	Calories: 142 | Fat: 13g | Carbs: 5.2g | Protein: 3.5g | Fiber: 2.4g
Day-6	Swiss-Style Italian Sausage	Simple Nutty Crepes	Sour Cream Salmon with Parmesan	German Fried Cabbage	Puffy Anise Cookies
	Calories:567 | Fat: 45g | Net Carbs: 7.6g | Protein: 34g	Calories: 260 | Fat: 21.7g | Carbs: 6.9g | Protein: 11.6g | Fiber: 3.8g	Calories:288 | Fat: 23.4g | Net Carbs: 1.2g | Protein: 16.2g	Calories: 243 | Fat: 22.2g | Carbs: 6.8g | Protein: 6.5g | Fiber: 1.9g	Calories: 142 | Fat: 13g | Carbs: 5.2g | Protein: 3.5g | Fiber: 2.4g
Day-7	Swiss-Style Italian Sausage	Puffy Anise Cookies	Sour Cream Salmon with Parmesan	German Fried Cabbage	Puffy Anise Cookies
	Calories:567 | Fat: 45g | Net Carbs: 7.6g | Protein: 34g	Calories: 142 | Fat: 13g | Carbs: 5.2g | Protein: 3.5g | Fiber: 2.4g	Calories:288 | Fat: 23.4g | Net Carbs: 1.2g | Protein: 16.2g	Calories: 243 | Fat: 22.2g | Carbs: 6.8g | Protein: 6.5g | Fiber: 1.9g	Calories: 142 | Fat: 13g | Carbs: 5.2g | Protein: 3.5g | Fiber: 2.4g

Chapter 3

Smoothies & Breakfasts

Asparagus & Goat Cheese Frittata

Prep time: 20 minutes | Cook time:17 minutes |Serves 4

- 4 tablespoons olive oil
- 1 onion, chopped
- 200 grams asparagus, chopped
- 8 large eggs, beaten
- 1 teaspoon habanero pepper, minced
- Salt and black pepper, to taste
- 250 grams goat cheese, crumbled
- 10 milliliters basil pesto
- 15 milliliters parsley, chopped

1. Preheat the oven to 190 degrees Celsius (370 degrees Fahrenheit).
2. Heat the olive oil in a frying pan over a medium heat. Add the onion and cook, stirring frequently, until softened and caramelized. Add the asparagus and cook for a further 5 minutes, or until tender.
3. Add the eggs, habanero pepper, salt, and black pepper to the frying pan. Cook, stirring gently, until the eggs are just set.
4. Scatter the goat cheese over the frittata. Transfer to the oven and bake for 12-15 minutes, or until the frittata is set in the middle.
5. Remove from the oven and let cool slightly. Slice into wedges and garnish with parsley and basil pesto.

PER SERVING

Calories:345 | Fat 27g | Net Carbs:5.2g | Protein 21.6g

Vanilla Lemon Crepes

Prep time: 25 minutes | Cook time: 8 minutes |Serves 4

- 125 milliliters almond milk, softened
- 4 large eggs
- ½ teaspoon granulated sweetener
- 125 grams almond flour
- 125 milliliters water
- 1 tablespoon lemon juice
- 1 tablespoon butter, melted
- 150 grams powdered sweetener

1. In a bowl, whisk together the almond milk, eggs, sweetener, and almond flour until smooth.
2. Heat a frying pan over a medium heat. Grease the pan with cooking spray or a little butter.
3. Pour a small amount of batter into the pan and cook for 2-3 minutes per side, or until golden brown. Repeat with the remaining batter.
4. In the same pan, melt the butter and add the powdered sweetener and water. Bring to a simmer and cook for 5-7 minutes, stirring constantly, until the syrup has thickened.
5. Add the lemon juice and stir to combine.
6. To serve, place a crepe on a plate and top with the lemon syrup. Enjoy!

PER SERVING

Calories:251 | Fat: 20g | Net Carbs:5.3g | Protein 7g

Hard-Boiled Eggs with Tuna & Chili Mayo

Prep time: 20 minutes | Cook time: 5 minutes |Serves 4

- 4 large eggs
- 400 grams canned tuna, drained
- 1 head of lettuce, shredded
- 2 spring onions, chopped
- 100 grams ricotta cheese, crumbled
- 40 milliliters sour cream
- ½ teaspoon mustard powder
- 125 milliliters mayonnaise
- ½ teaspoon lemon juice
- ½ teaspoon chilli powder
- 2 dill pickles, sliced
- Salt and black pepper, to taste

1. Bring a pan of water to the boil. Add the eggs and cook for 10 minutes, then remove from the heat and plunge into cold water to cool. Once cool, peel and chop the eggs.
2. In a large bowl, combine the tuna, eggs, spring onions, ricotta cheese, lettuce, sour cream, mustard powder, mayonnaise, lemon juice, chilli powder, salt, and pepper. Stir to combine well.
3. Serve in a serving platter, topped with dill pickle slices.

PER SERVING

Calories:311 | Fat 19.5g | Net Carbs:1.5g | Protein 31g

Almond & Raspberries Cakes

Prep time: 30 minutes | Cook time: 5 minutes |Serves 4

- 250 grams almond flour
- 2 teaspoons baking powder
- 1 teaspoon vanilla extract
- 2 tablespoons almond flakes
- ½ teaspoon salt
- 2 tablespoons sweetener of choice
- 225 grams cream cheese, softened
- 60 milliliters butter, melted
- 1 large egg
- 10 raspberries
- 250 milliliters unsweetened almond milk

1. Mash the raspberries with a fork and set aside. In a large bowl, whisk together the almond flour, baking powder, and salt. In a separate bowl, beat the cream cheese, sweetener, and butter until smooth. Whisk in the egg and almond milk.
2. Fold in the flour mixture and mashed raspberries. Spoon the batter into greased muffin cups two-thirds full. Bake in a preheated oven at 200 degrees Celsius (400 degrees Fahrenheit) for 20 minutes, or until a toothpick inserted into the center comes out clean.
3. Allow the cakes to cool in the muffin cups for a few minutes before transferring them to a wire rack to cool completely.

PER SERVING

Calories:353 | Fat: 32.6g | Net Carbs:8.6g | Protein 9.4g

Broccoli, Egg & Pancetta Gratin

Prep time: 25 minutes | Cook time: 7 minutes |Serves 4

- 1 head broccoli, cut into florets
- 1 red bell pepper, chopped
- 4 rashers of pancetta, chopped
- 4 tablespoons olive oil
- 1 teaspoon dried oregano
- Salt and black pepper to taste
- 6 large eggs
- 150 grams grated Parmesan cheese

1. Line a baking sheet with baking parchment and preheat the oven to 220 degrees Celsius (420 degrees Fahrenheit).
2. Heat the olive oil in a frying pan over a medium heat. Add the pancetta and cook, stirring frequently, for about 3 minutes, or until crisp.
3. Arrange the broccoli, bell pepper, and pancetta on the baking sheet in a single layer. Season with salt, oregano, and black pepper. Bake for 10 minutes, or until the vegetables have softened.
4. Remove the baking sheet from the oven and make four indentations in the vegetables. Crack an egg into each indentation. Sprinkle with Parmesan cheese.
5. Return the baking sheet to the oven and bake for a further 5-7 minutes, or until the egg whites are firm and the cheese has melted.

PER SERVING

Calories:464 | Fat: 38g | Net Carbs:4.2g | Protein 24g

Chicken Salad with Parmesan

Prep time: 30 minutes | Cook time: 4 minutes | Serves 4

- For the chicken:
- 250 grams skinless, boneless chicken thighs
- 60 milliliters lemon juice
- 2 garlic cloves, minced
- 4 tablespoons olive oil
- For the salad:
- 1 head of romaine lettuce, shredded
- 3 Parmesan crisps
- Parmesan cheese, grated
- Dressing:
- 40 milliliters extra virgin olive oil
- 15 milliliters lemon juice
- Salt and black pepper to taste

1. In a Ziploc bag, combine the chicken, lemon juice, olive oil, and garlic. Seal the bag, shake to combine, and refrigerate for 1 hour.
2. Preheat a grill to medium heat and grill the chicken for about 4 minutes per side, or until cooked through.
3. In a small bowl, combine the dressing ingredients and mix well. On a serving platter, arrange the lettuce and Parmesan crisps.
4. Drizzle the dressing over the lettuce and toss to coat. Top with the chicken and grated Parmesan cheese to serve.

PER SERVING

Calories:529 | Fat: 36.5g | Net Carbs:4.3g | Protein 34g

Smoked Salmon, Bacon & Poached Egg Salad

Prep time: 15 minutes | Cook time: 9 minutes |Serves 4

- 6 large eggs
- 1 head of romaine lettuce, shredded
- 100 grams smoked salmon, chopped
- 6 rashers of bacon, cooked and crumbled
- Salt and black pepper, to taste
- Dressing:
- 125 milliliters mayonnaise
- ½ teaspoon garlic puree
- 15 milliliters lemon juice
- 1 teaspoon Tabasco sauce

1. In a bowl, whisk together the dressing ingredients and set aside.
2. Bring a pot of salted water to the boil. Crack each egg into a small bowl and gently slide into the water. Poach for 2 to 3 minutes, remove with a slotted spoon, transfer to a paper towel to drain, and plate. Poach the remaining eggs.
3. Fry the bacon in a frying pan over medium heat until browned and crispy, about 6 minutes, turning once. Remove, allow to cool, and chop into small pieces.
4. Toss the lettuce, smoked salmon, bacon, and dressing in a salad bowl.
5. Divide the salad onto plates, top with the eggs each, and serve immediately or chilled.

PER SERVING

Calories:452 | Fat: 36.9g | Net Carbs: 4.4g | Protein 26.7g

Morning Berry-Green Smoothie

Prep time: 5 minutes | Cook time: 5 minutes | Serves 4

- 1 ripe avocado, halved and stoned
- 3 cups mixed blueberries and strawberries
- 500ml unsweetened almond milk
- 120ml double cream
- 2 teaspoons erythritol
- 1 cup ice cubes
- 75g mixed nuts and seeds

1. Combine the avocado, blueberries, strawberries, almond milk, double cream, erythritol, ice cubes, and nuts and seeds in a blender.
2. Blend on high speed until smooth and uniform.
3. Pour the smoothie into glasses and serve immediately.

PER SERVING

Calories:360 | Fat: 33.3g | Net Carbs: 6g | Protein: 6g

Egg Tofu Scramble with Kale & Mushrooms

Prep time: 30 minutes | Cook time: 13 minutes | Serves 4

- 2 tablespoons ghee
- 1 cup sliced white mushrooms
- 2 cloves garlic, minced
- 450g firm tofu, pressed and crumbled
- Salt and black pepper to taste
- 1/2 cup thinly sliced kale
- 6 large eggs

1. Melt the ghee in a non-stick frying pan over a medium heat. Sauté the mushrooms for 5 minutes, or until they have lost their liquid. Add the garlic and cook for 1 minute.
2. Crumble the tofu into the pan and season with salt and black pepper. Cook, stirring continuously, for 6 minutes. Add the kale in batches and cook until softened, about 7 minutes.
3. Crack the eggs into a bowl and whisk until well combined. Pour the eggs over the kale and tofu and use a spatula to stir immediately, scrambling the eggs as they cook. Cook for about 5 minutes, or until the eggs are scrambled and no longer runny.
4. Serve immediately with low carb crusted bread.

PER SERVING

Calories:469 | Fat: 39g | Net Carbs: 5g | Protein: 25g

Vegetable Keto Bread

Prep time: 70 minutes | Cook time: 55 minutes |Serves 4

- 250 grams pumpkin, grated
- 250 grams zucchini, grated
- 150 grams coconut flour
- 6 large eggs
- 2 tablespoons olive oil
- 1.5 teaspoons baking soda
- 20 grams ground cinnamon
- 1 teaspoon salt
- 125 milliliters buttermilk
- 1 teaspoon apple cider vinegar

1. Preheat oven to 180 degrees Celsius (360 degrees Fahrenheit). Grease and line a loaf pan with baking parchment.
2. In a large bowl, combine the pumpkin, zucchini, coconut flour, eggs, olive oil, baking soda, cinnamon, salt, buttermilk, and apple cider vinegar. Stir until well combined.
3. Pour the batter into the prepared loaf pan and bake for 55 minutes, or until a toothpick inserted into the center comes out clean. 4. Let the bread cool in the pan for 5 minutes before removing it to a wire rack to cool completely.

PER SERVING

Calories:283 | Fat: 17g | Net Carbs:3.5g | Protein 13g

Smoked Salmon Rolls with Dill Cream Cheese

Prep time: 10 minutes | Cook time: 5 minutes | Serves 3

- 75g cream cheese, softened
- 1 small lemon, zested and juiced
- 1 tablespoon chopped fresh dill
- Salt and black pepper to taste
- 3 (18cm) low carb tortillas
- 12 slices smoked salmon

1. In a bowl, mix the cream cheese, lemon juice, zest, dill, salt, and black pepper.
2. Place a tortilla on a sheet of plastic wrap. Spread the cream cheese mixture over the tortilla, leaving a 1-inch border. Top with 6 slices of smoked salmon. Roll up the tortilla tightly, starting from the long edge. Wrap the tortilla in the plastic wrap and refrigerate for at least 2 hours.
3. Remove the tortillas from the refrigerator and unwrap them. Cut each tortilla into 6 wheels. Serve immediately.

PER SERVING

Calories:250 | Fat: 16g | Net Carbs: 7g | Protein: 18g

Warm Beef Salad

Prep time: 5 minutes | Cook time: 20 minutes |Serves 5

- 4 tablespoons olive oil, divided
- 900 grams beef strips
- 250 milliliters ale
- 4 garlic cloves, sliced
- 1 celery stalk, sliced
- 4 scallions, chopped
- 500 grams cabbage, shredded
- 1 tablespoon fresh lime juice
- 4 tablespoons toasted sesame seeds

1. Heat 2 tablespoons of the olive oil in a large soup pot over a medium-high heat. Cook the beef to your liking.
2. Add in the ale, garlic, and celery. Reduce the heat to medium-low and simmer, partially covered, for 10 minutes.
3. Garnish with toasted sesame seeds and serve immediately.

PER SERVING

Calories: 321 | Fat: 11.8g | Carbs: 5.8g | Protein: 43.6g | Fiber: 1.9g

Egg in a Cheesy Spinach Nests

Prep time: 35 minutes | Cook time: 17 minutes | Serves 4

- 2 tablespoons olive oil
- 1 clove garlic, grated
- 225g spinach, chopped
- Salt and black pepper to taste
- 2 tablespoons grated Parmesan cheese
- 2 tablespoons grated Gouda cheese
- 4 large eggs

1. Preheat the oven to 175 degrees Celsius (350 degrees Fahrenheit). Heat the olive oil in a non-stick frying pan over a medium heat. Add the garlic and cook for 2 minutes, or until softened.
2. Grease a baking sheet with cooking spray. Using your hands, make 4 nests out of the spinach, pressing them down firmly into the baking sheet. Crack an egg into each nest. Sprinkle with the Parmesan and Gouda cheeses.
3. Bake for 15 minutes, or until the egg whites have set and the yolks are still runny. Serve immediately with low carb toasts and coffee.

PER SERVING

Calories:230 | Fat: 17.5g | Net Carbs: 4g | Protein: 12g

Chapter 4

Poultry Recipes

Chicken Sausage and Mozzarella Omelet

Prep time: 15 minutes | Cook time: 7 minutes | Serves 1

- 2 large eggs
- 6 basil leaves
- 50g mozzarella cheese, grated
- 1 tablespoon butter
- 1 tablespoon water
- 5-8 thin chicken sausage slices
- 5 thin tomato slices
- Salt and black pepper to taste

1. Whisk the eggs together with the water, salt, and pepper.
2. Melt the butter in a frying pan over a medium heat. Add the eggs and cook for 30 seconds, or until the bottom is set.
3. Spread the chicken sausage slices over the eggs, followed by the tomato slices and mozzarella cheese.
4. Cover the pan and cook for a further 3 minutes, or until the eggs are completely set.
5. Remove the pan from the heat and run a spatula around the edges of the omelette. Carefully flip the omelette onto a warm plate, folded side down.
6. Garnish with the basil leaves and serve with a green salad.

PER SERVING

Calories:451 | Net Carbs: 3g | Fat: 36.5g | Protein 30g

Rosemary Chicken with Avocado Sauce

Prep time: 22 minutes | Cook time: 12 minutes |Serves 4

FOR THE SAUCE:
- 60 milliliters mayonnaise
- 1 ripe avocado, mashed
- 15 milliliters lemon juice
- Salt to taste

FOR THE CHICKEN:
- 4 tablespoons olive oil
- 200 grams skinless, boneless chicken breasts
- Salt and black pepper to taste
- 50 grams rosemary, chopped
- 60 milliliters warm water

1. To make the sauce, mash the avocado with a fork in a bowl. Add the mayonnaise and lemon juice and season with salt to taste.
2. Heat the olive oil in a large skillet over a medium heat. Season the chicken breasts with salt and black pepper and cook for 4 minutes on each side, or until golden brown. Remove the chicken to a plate.
3. Pour the warm water into the same skillet and add the rosemary. Bring to a simmer for 3 minutes, then add the chicken. Cover and cook on low heat for 5 minutes, or until the liquid has reduced and the chicken is cooked through.
4. Dish the chicken into serving plates and spoon the avocado sauce over.

PER SERVING

Calories:406 | Fat: 34.1g | Net Carbs: 3.9g | Protein 22.3g

Chicken & Cheese Filled Avocados

Prep time: 10 minutes | Cook time: 5 minutes |Serves 2

- 375 grams cooked and shredded chicken
- 2 ripe avocados, mashed
- 60 milliliters mayonnaise
- 1 teaspoon dried thyme
- 30 grams cream cheese, softened
- Salt and black pepper, to taste
- ¼ teaspoon cayenne pepper
- ½ teaspoon onion powder
- ½ teaspoon garlic powder
- 1 teaspoon paprika
- Salt and black pepper, to taste
- 40 milliliters lemon juice

1. Halve the avocados and scoop out the flesh. Place the flesh in a bowl and add the chicken. Stir in the remaining ingredients.
2. Fill the avocado cups with the chicken mixture and serve.

PER SERVING

Calories:518 | Fat: 41.6 | Net Carbs: 5.3g | Protein 23.2g

Green Bean & Broccoli Chicken Stir-Fry

Prep time: 30 minutes | Cook time: 25 minutes |Serves 4

- 200 grams skinless, boneless chicken breasts, sliced
- 4 tablespoons olive oil
- 1 teaspoon red pepper flakes
- 1 teaspoon onion powder
- 20 grams fresh ginger, grated
- 60 milliliters tamari sauce
- ½ teaspoon garlic powder
- 125 milliliters water
- 100 grams xylitol
- 50 grams green beans, chopped
- ½ teaspoon xanthan gum
- 50 grams green onions, chopped
- 100 grams broccoli, cut into florets

1. Steam the green beans in salted water for 2-3 minutes. Heat the olive oil in a large skillet over a medium heat. Add the chicken and ginger and cook for 4 minutes, or until browned.
2. Stir in the water, onion powder, red pepper flakes, garlic powder, tamari sauce, xanthan gum, and xylitol. Cook for 15 minutes, or until the sauce has thickened.
3. Add the green onions, green beans, and broccoli and cook for a further 6 minutes, or until the vegetables are tender.

PER SERVING

Calories:411 | Fat: 24.5g | Net Carbs: 6.2g | Protein 28.3g

Winter Chicken with Vegetables

Prep time: 35 minutes | Cook time: 30 minutes |Serves 4

- 2 tablespoons olive oil
- 500ml double cream
- 450g boneless, skinless chicken breasts, chopped
- 1 onion, chopped
- 1 carrot, chopped
- 200ml chicken stock
- Salt and black pepper, to taste
- 1 bay leaf
- 1 turnip, chopped
- 1 parsnip, chopped
- 100g green beans, chopped
- 3 teaspoons fresh thyme, chopped

1. Heat a large saucepan over a medium heat. Add the olive oil and onion and cook for 3 minutes, or until softened. Add the stock, carrot, turnip, parsnip, chicken, and bay leaf. Bring to a boil, then reduce the heat and simmer for 20 minutes, or until the chicken is cooked through.
2. Add the green beans and cook for a further 7 minutes, or until tender. Discard the bay leaf.
3. Stir in the double cream and season with salt and pepper to taste. Scatter with the fresh thyme to serve.

PER SERVING

Calories:483 | Fat: 32.5g | Net Carbs: 6.9g | Protein 33g

Pancetta & Cheese Stuffed Chicken

Prep time: 40 minutes | Cook time: 23 minutes |Serves 4

- 4 slices pancetta
- 2 tablespoons olive oil
- 4 boneless, skinless chicken breasts
- 1 garlic clove, minced
- 1 shallot, finely chopped
- 2 tablespoons dried oregano
- 4 ounces mascarpone cheese
- 1 lemon, zested
- Salt and black pepper, to taste

1. Heat the oil in a small frying pan over a medium heat. Add the garlic and shallots and cook for 3 minutes, or until softened. Stir in the salt, pepper, and lemon zest. Transfer to a bowl and let cool. Stir in the mascarpone cheese and oregano.
2. Make a pocket in each chicken breast by slicing horizontally through the centre, being careful not to cut all the way through. Fill the pockets with the cheese mixture and fold the chicken back together. Wrap each breast with two slices of pancetta and secure the ends with toothpicks.
3. Place the chicken on a greased baking sheet and bake in a preheated oven at 190 degrees Celsius (380 degrees Fahrenheit) for 20 minutes, or until the chicken is cooked through and the pancetta is crispy.

PER SERVING

Calories:643 | Fat: 44.5g | Net Carbs: 6.2g | Protein 52.8g

Grilled Chicken and Vegetable Kabobs

Prep time: 5 minutes | Cook time: 20 minutes |Serves 6

- 3 tablespoons olive oil
- 6 tablespoons dry sherry
- 1 tablespoon wholegrain mustard
- 750 grams skinless, boneless chicken, cut into cubes
- 2 red onions, cut into wedges
- 1 green bell pepper, cut into 1-inch pieces
- 1 red bell pepper, cut into 1-inch pieces
- 1 yellow bell pepper, cut into 1-inch pieces
- 1/2 teaspoon sea salt
- 1/4 teaspoon black pepper, or more to taste

1. In a large bowl, combine the olive oil, dry sherry, mustard, and chicken. Mix well to coat.
2. Skewer the chicken and vegetables alternately, until all the ingredients are used. Season with salt and pepper.
3. Preheat your grill to medium-high heat.
4. Place the kabobs on the grill and cook, turning every 2 minutes, for 15-20 minutes, or until the chicken is cooked through and the vegetables are tender.
5. Serve warm.

PER SERVING

Calories: 200 | Fat: 8.1g | Carbs: 7g | Protein: 24.3g | Fiber: 1.3g

Capocollo-Wrapped Chicken

Prep time: 5 minutes | Cook time: 40 minutes |Serves 5

- 900 grams chicken drumsticks, skinless and boneless
- 1 garlic clove, peeled and halved
- 1/2 teaspoon smoked paprika
- Sea salt and black pepper, to taste
- 15 thin slices of capocollo

1. Using a sharp knife, butterfly cut the chicken drumsticks in half.
2. Lay each chicken drumstick flat on a chopping board and rub the garlic halves over the surface of the chicken drumsticks. Season with paprika, salt, and pepper.
3. Lay a slice of capocollo on each piece, pressing lightly. Roll them up and secure with cocktail sticks.
4. Preheat your oven to 218 degrees Celsius.
5. Bake in the preheated oven for 15 minutes, or until the edges of the chicken begin to brown.
6. Turn over and bake for a further 15-20 minutes, or until the chicken is cooked through.
7. Serve immediately.

PER SERVING

Calories: 485 | Fat: 33.8g | Carbs: 3.6g | Protein: 39.2g | Fiber: 1g

Sunday Chicken Bake

Prep time: 5 minutes | Cook time: 30 minutes |Serves 6

- 1 tablespoon olive oil
- 300 grams chicken breast fillets, chopped into bite-sized chunks
- 2 garlic cloves, sliced
- 1/4 teaspoon Korean chili pepper flakes
- 1/4 teaspoon Himalayan salt
- 1/2 teaspoon poultry seasoning mix
- 1 red bell pepper, deseeded and chopped
- 2 ripe tomatoes, chopped
- 1/4 cup double cream
- 1/4 cup sour cream

1. Preheat your oven to 199 degrees Celsius.
2. Brush a casserole dish with olive oil. Add the chicken, garlic, Korean chili pepper flakes, salt, and poultry seasoning mix to the casserole dish.
3. Layer the red bell pepper and tomatoes on top of the chicken.
4. In a small bowl, whisk together the double cream and sour cream.
5. Pour the cream mixture over the chicken and vegetables.
6. Bake in the preheated oven for 25 minutes, or until the chicken is cooked through.
7. Serve immediately.

PER SERVING

Calories: 410 | Fat: 20.7g | Carbs: 6.2g | Protein: 50g | Fiber: 1.5g

Primavera Stuffed Turkey Fillets

Prep time: 5 minutes | Cook time: 1 hour |Serves 6

- 3 tablespoons extra-virgin olive oil
- 1 tablespoon Italian seasoning mix
- Sea salt and black pepper, to taste
- 4 garlic cloves, sliced
- 180 grams Asiago cheese, sliced
- 2 bell peppers, thinly sliced
- 750 grams turkey breasts
- 2 tablespoons Italian parsley, roughly chopped

1. Preheat your oven to 180 degrees Celsius. Brush the sides and bottom of a casserole dish with 2 tablespoons of extra-virgin olive oil.
2. Sprinkle the turkey breasts with the Italian seasoning mix, salt, and black pepper on all sides.
3. Make slits in each turkey breast and stuff with the garlic, cheese, and bell peppers. Drizzle the turkey breasts with the remaining tablespoon of olive oil.
4. Bake in the preheated oven for 50 minutes, or until an instant-read thermometer registers 74 degrees Celsius.
5. Garnish with Italian parsley and serve warm.

PER SERVING

Calories: 347 | Fat: 22.2g | Carbs: 3g | Protein: 32g | Fiber: 0.5g

Mediterranean Roasted Chicken with Aromatics

Prep time: 5 minutes | Cook time: 25 minutes |Serves 5

- 3 tablespoons olive oil
- 750 grams chicken drumettes
- 2 garlic cloves, minced
- 1 thyme sprig
- 1 rosemary sprig
- 1/2 teaspoon dried oregano
- Sea salt and black pepper, to taste
- 2 tablespoons Greek cooking wine
- 125 milliliters chicken bone broth
- 1 red onion, cut into wedges
- 1 bell pepper, sliced

1. Preheat your oven to 218 degrees Celsius. Brush the sides and bottom of a baking dish with 2 tablespoons of olive oil.
2. Heat the remaining tablespoon of olive oil in a frying pan over a medium heat. Brown the chicken drumettes for 5-6 minutes per side.
3. Transfer the warm chicken drumettes to the baking dish. Add the garlic, thyme, rosemary, oregano, wine, and broth. Scatter the red onion and bell pepper around the chicken drumettes.
4. Roast in the preheated oven for 13 minutes, or until the chicken is cooked through.
5. Serve immediately.

PER SERVING

Calories: 218| Fat: 9.1g | Carbs: 4.2g | Protein: 28.6g | Fiber: 0.7g

Crispy Chicken Filets in Tomato Sauce

Prep time: 5 minutes | Cook time: 15 minutes |Serves 3

- 3 tablespoons double cream
- 1 egg
- 50 grams pork rinds, crushed
- 50 grams Romano cheese, grated
- Sea salt and black pepper, to taste
- 1 teaspoon cayenne pepper
- 1 teaspoon dried parsley
- 1 garlic clove, halved
- 250 grams chicken fillets
- 4 tablespoons olive oil
- 1 large-sized Roma tomato, pureed

1. In a large bowl, whisk together the double cream and egg.
2. In a separate bowl, combine the crushed pork rinds, Romano cheese, salt, pepper, cayenne pepper, and dried parsley.
3. Rub the garlic halves all over the chicken fillets. Dip the chicken fillets in the egg mixture, then coat with the breading on all sides.
4. Heat the olive oil in a large frying pan over a medium-high heat. Once hot, cook the chicken fillets for 2-4 minutes on each side, or until cooked through.
5. Transfer the cooked chicken fillets to a baking dish that has been lightly greased with non-stick cooking spray. Pour the pureed tomato over the chicken fillets.
6. Bake in the oven at 180 degrees Celsius for 2-3 minutes, or until the tomato sauce is heated through.
7. Serve immediately.

PER SERVING

Calories: 359 | Fat: 23.6g | Carbs: 5.8g | Fiber: 1.2g | Protein: 30.4g

Chapter 5

Pork, Beef & Lamb Recipes

Tart with Meat & Mashed Cauliflower

Prep time: 1 hour and 40 minutes | Cook time: 60 minutes | Serves 8

FOR THE CRUST:

- 1 egg
- 4 tablespoons melted butter
- 225 grams almond flour
- ¼ teaspoon xanthan gum
- 40 grams grated mozzarella cheese
- A pinch of salt

FOR THE FILLING:

- 900 grams ground pork
- 80 grams onion, pureed
- 1.125 teaspoons allspice
- 250 grams mashed cauliflower
- 15 grams ground sage
- 40 grams butter

1. Preheat the oven to 180 degrees Celsius (350 degrees Fahrenheit).
2. In a bowl, whisk together the egg, butter, almond flour, xanthan gum, mozzarella cheese, and salt. Form two balls of dough and refrigerate for 10 minutes.
3. Melt the butter in a frying pan over medium heat and add the ground pork. Cook for about 10 minutes, stirring occasionally. Remove to a bowl and stir in the onion, allspice, cauliflower, sage, and butter.
4. Roll out one of the dough balls and place it in the bottom of a greased 9-inch tart tin. Spread the filling over the crust and top with the other dough ball.
5. Bake in the preheated oven for 50 minutes, or until the crust is golden brown and the filling is cooked through.
6. Serve warm or cold.

PER SERVING

Calories:485 | Net Carbs: 4g | Fat: 41g | Protein 29g

Roasted Pork Stuffed with Ham & Cheese

Prep time: 40 minutes | Cook time: 27 minutes | Serves 4

- 2 tablespoons olive oil
- Zest and juice of 1 lime
- 1 garlic clove, minced
- 2 tablespoons fresh cilantro, chopped
- 2 tablespoons fresh mint, chopped
- Salt and black pepper, to taste
- 1 teaspoon cumin
- 2 pork loin steaks
- 1 pickle, chopped
- 2 ounces smoked ham, sliced
- 2 ounces Gruyère cheese, sliced
- 1 tablespoon mustard

1. To make the marinade, combine the lime zest, oil, black pepper, cumin, cilantro, lime juice, garlic, mint, and salt in a food processor. Place the steaks in the marinade and toss to coat. Set aside in the refrigerator for at least 30 minutes, or up to overnight.
2. Preheat the oven to 180 degrees Celsius (350 degrees Fahrenheit).
3. Remove the steaks from the marinade and arrange on a work surface. Top each steak with the pickle, mustard, cheese, and ham. Roll up the steaks and secure with toothpicks.
4. Heat a frying pan over medium heat. Add the rolled steaks and cook for 2 minutes per side, or until browned. Transfer the steaks to a baking sheet and bake in the preheated oven for 25 minutes, or until cooked through.
5. Serve warm.

PER SERVING

Calories:433 | Fat: 38g | Net Carbs: 4.2g | Protein 24g

Pork Kofte with Tomato Passata & Basil

Prep time: 45 minutes | Cook time: 33 minutes |Serves 4

- 450 grams ground pork
- 1 tablespoon olive oil
- 1 tablespoon crushed pork scratchings
- 1 garlic clove, minced
- 1 shallot, chopped
- 1 small egg
- ⅓ teaspoon paprika
- Salt and black pepper, to taste
- 1 tablespoon chopped parsley
- ½ cup sugar-free tomato sauce
- ½ teaspoon oregano
- ⅓ cup Italian-style grated cheese
- 1 tablespoon chopped basil, to garnish

1. In a bowl, combine the ground pork, shallot, pork rinds, garlic, egg, paprika, oregano, parsley, salt, and black pepper. Mix just until combined. Form into meatballs and place in an oiled baking dish. Drizzle with olive oil.
2. Bake in a preheated oven at 190 degrees Celsius (390 degrees Fahrenheit) for 18 minutes.
3. Pour the tomato sauce over the meatballs. Sprinkle with the Italian blend cheeses and bake for a further 10-15 minutes, or until the cheese has melted.
4. Remove from the oven and garnish with basil. Serve with cauliflower mash.

PER SERVING

Calories:586 | Fat: 38g | Net Carbs: 7.3g | Protein 39.2g

Caramelized Onion over Pork Burgers

Prep time: 20 minutes | Cook time: 10 minutes |Serves 4

- 2 tablespoons olive oil
- 450 grams ground pork
- Salt and black pepper, to taste
- ½ teaspoon chili powder
- 1 tablespoon chopped parsley
- 1 white onion, sliced into rings
- ½ tablespoon balsamic vinegar
- 1 drop liquid stevia
- 1 tomato, sliced into rings
- 1 tablespoon mayonnaise

1. Heat half of the olive oil in a frying pan over medium heat. Add the onion rings and cook for 2 minutes. Stir in the balsamic vinegar and liquid stevia. Cook for a further 30 seconds, stirring occasionally, until the onions are caramelized. Remove to a plate.
2. In a bowl, combine the ground pork, salt, pepper, chili powder, and parsley. Mix well. Form into 2 patties.
3. Heat the remaining olive oil in the frying pan over medium heat. Cook the patties for 4-5 minutes per side, or until cooked through. Remove to a plate and let rest for 3 minutes.
4. To assemble the burgers, place a tomato slice on a plate. Spread with mayonnaise and top with a patty. Add some caramelized onions and top with another tomato slice. Serve immediately.

PER SERVING

Calories:510 | Fat: 41.2g | Net Carbs: 2.6g | Protein 31g

Garlicky Pork with Bell Peppers

Prep time: 40 minutes | Cook time: 14 minutes | Serves 4

- 40g butter
- 4 bone-in pork steaks
- 250ml chicken stock
- Salt and black pepper, to taste
- A pinch of lemon pepper
- 30ml olive oil
- 10 garlic cloves, minced
- 2 tablespoons fresh parsley, chopped
- 4 bell peppers, sliced
- 1 lemon, sliced

1. Heat a large skillet over medium heat. Add 20g butter and 20g olive oil. Season the pork steaks with salt and pepper. Cook the pork steaks for 5 minutes on each side, or until browned. Remove the pork steaks from the pan and set aside.
2. Add the remaining butter and olive oil to the pan. Add the garlic and bell peppers and cook for 4 minutes, or until softened.
3. Pour in the chicken stock, lemon slices, salt, lemon pepper, and black pepper. Bring to a simmer and cook for 5 minutes.
4. Return the pork steaks to the pan and cook for 10 minutes, or until cooked through.
5. Divide the pork steaks and sauce among plates and sprinkle with parsley to serve.

PER SERVING

Calories:456 | Fat: 25g | Net Carbs: 6g | Protein: 40g

Oregano Pork Chops with Spicy Tomato Sauce

Prep time: 50 minutes | Cook time: 36 minutes | Serves 4

- 4 boneless, skinless pork chops
- 1 tablespoon fresh oregano, chopped
- 2 garlic cloves, minced
- 15g canola oil
- 400g canned diced tomatoes
- 1 tablespoon tomato paste
- Salt and black pepper, to taste
- 100ml tomato juice
- 1 red chili, finely chopped

1. Heat the oil in a large skillet over medium heat. Season the pork chops with salt and pepper. Cook the pork chops for 6 minutes on each side, or until browned. Remove to a plate and set aside.
2. Add the garlic to the skillet and cook for 30 seconds. Stir in the tomato paste, tomatoes, tomato juice, and chili. Bring to a boil, then reduce the heat to low and simmer for 20 minutes.
3. Return the pork chops to the skillet and cook for 10 minutes, or until cooked through. Remove the pork chops to plates and sprinkle with fresh oregano to serve.

PER SERVING

Calories:410 | Fat: 21g | Net Carbs: 3.6g | Protein: 39g

Creamy Reuben Soup

Prep time: 20 minutes| Cook time: 19 minutes | Serves 6

- 1 onion, diced
- 1.75 liters beef stock
- 1 teaspoon caraway seeds
- 2 celery stalks, diced
- 2 garlic cloves, minced
- 6.25 grams black pepper
- 500 ml heavy cream
- 250 ml sauerkraut
- 450 g corned beef, chopped
- 30 grams butter
- 375 g Swiss cheese
- Salt and black pepper, to taste

1. Melt the butter in a large saucepan over a medium heat. Add the onion and celery and cook for 3 minutes, or until softened. Add the garlic and cook for a further minute.
2. Pour in the beef stock, sauerkraut, salt, caraway seeds, and a pinch of pepper. Bring to a boil, then reduce the heat to low and simmer for 15 minutes.
3. Stir in the heavy cream and Swiss cheese and cook for a further minute, or until the cheese has melted. Season with salt and pepper to taste.

PER SERVING

Calories:450 | Net Carbs: 8g | Fat: 37g | Protein 23g

Asian Spiced Beef with Broccoli

Prep time: 30 minutes | Cook time: 20 minutes |Serves 4

- 125 milliliters coconut milk
- 4 tablespoons coconut oil
- 1 teaspoon garlic powder
- 1 teaspoon onion powder
- 12.5 milliliters coconut aminos
- 450 grams beef steak, cut into strips
- Salt and black pepper, to taste
- 1 head broccoli, cut into florets
- 15 milliliters Thai green curry paste
- 5 milliliters ginger paste
- 15 milliliters cilantro, chopped
- 15 milliliters sesame seeds

1. Heat the coconut oil in a large skillet over medium heat.
2. Add the beef and season with garlic powder, pepper, salt, ginger paste, and onion powder. Cook for 4 minutes, or until browned.
3. Stir in the broccoli and cook for 5 minutes, or until tender.
4. Pour in the coconut milk, coconut aminos, and Thai curry paste. Bring to a boil, then reduce heat and simmer for 15 minutes, or until the sauce has thickened.
5. Serve sprinkled with cilantro and sesame seeds.

PER SERVING

Calories:623 | Fat: 43.2g | Net Carbs: 2.3g | Protein 53.5g

Beef Steaks with Creamy Bacon & Mushrooms

Prep time: 50 minutes | Cook time: 40 minutes |Serves 4

- 50 grams bacon, chopped
- 250 grams mushrooms, sliced
- 1 garlic clove, chopped
- 1 shallot, chopped
- 250 milliliters heavy cream
- 450 grams beef steaks
- 1 teaspoon ground nutmeg
- 4 tablespoons coconut oil
- Salt and black pepper, to taste
- 15 milliliters parsley, chopped

1. In a frying pan over medium heat, cook the bacon for 2-3 minutes, or until crisp. Remove from the pan and set aside.
2. Heat the coconut oil in the same pan over medium heat. Add the onions, garlic, and mushrooms and cook for 4 minutes, or until softened.
3. Stir in the beef, season with salt, pepper, and nutmeg, and sear until browned on both sides.
4. Preheat the oven to 180 degrees Celsius (360 degrees Fahrenheit).
5. Transfer the pan to the oven and bake for 25 minutes, or until the beef is cooked to your liking.
6. Remove the beef from the pan and set aside to rest.
7. Place the pan over medium heat, pour in the heavy cream over the mushroom mixture, and add the reserved bacon. Cook for 5 minutes, or until the sauce has thickened.
8. Serve the beef steaks topped with the creamy bacon and mushroom sauce. Sprinkle with parsley and serve.

PER SERVING

Calories:765 | Fat: 71g | Net Carbs: 3.8g | Protein 32g

Veggie Chuck Roast Beef

Prep time: 1 hour 40 minutes | Cook time: 1 hour 35 minutes |Serves 4

- 4 tablespoons olive oil
- 450 grams beef chuck roast, cubed
- 250 milliliters canned diced tomatoes
- 1 carrot, chopped
- Salt and black pepper, to taste
- 250 grams mushrooms, sliced
- 1 celery stalk, chopped
- 1 red bell pepper, sliced
- 1 onion, chopped
- 1 bay leaf
- 125 milliliters beef stock
- 15 milliliters fresh rosemary, chopped
- 1/2 teaspoon dry mustard
- 1 tablespoon almond flour

1. Preheat the oven to 180 degrees Celsius (350 degrees Fahrenheit).
2. Heat the olive oil in a large pot over medium heat. Brown the beef on all sides for 4-5 minutes.
3. Stir in the tomatoes, onion, mustard, carrot, mushrooms, bell pepper, celery, and stock. Season with salt and pepper.
4. In a bowl, whisk together 125 milliliters of water and the almond flour. Add to the pot and stir to combine.
5. Transfer the pot to a baking dish and bake for 90 minutes, stirring at intervals of 30 minutes.
6. Sprinkle with rosemary and serve warm.

PER SERVING

Calories:325 | Fat: 17.8g | Net Carbs:5.6g | Protein 31.5g

Beef, Broccoli & Rosemary Slow-Cooked Stew

Prep time: 4 hours 15 minutes | Cook time: 4 hours |Serves 4

- 4 tablespoons olive oil
- 450 grams ground beef
- 125 milliliters leeks, chopped
- 1 head broccoli, cut into florets
- Salt and black pepper, to taste
- 1 teaspoon yellow mustard
- 1 teaspoon Worcestershire sauce
- 2 tomatoes, chopped
- 250 milliliters tomato sauce
- 15 milliliters fresh rosemary, chopped
- 1/2 teaspoon dried oregano

1. Coat the broccoli with salt and pepper. Place in a bowl, drizzle with olive oil, and toss to combine.
2. In a separate bowl, combine the beef, Worcestershire sauce, leeks, salt, mustard, and black pepper. Stir well.
3. Press the beef mixture into the bottom of a slow cooker.
4. Scatter the broccoli florets on top of the beef mixture.
5. Add the tomatoes, tomato sauce, oregano, and rosemary.
6. Cook on high for 4 hours, or until the beef is cooked through and the broccoli is tender.
7. Serve hot, sprinkled with additional rosemary.

PER SERVING

Calories:677 | Fat: 42.1g | Net Carbs: 8.3g | Protein 63g

Jerked Beef Stew

Prep time: 1 hour 10 minutes | Cook time: 1 hour 6 minutes |Serves 4

- 1 onion, chopped
- 4 tablespoons olive oil
- 1 teaspoon ginger paste
- 1 teaspoon soy sauce
- 450 grams beef stew meat, cubed
- 1 red bell pepper, seeded and chopped
- 1/2 scotch bonnet pepper, chopped
- 2 green chilies, chopped
- 250 milliliters tomatoes, chopped
- 15 milliliters fresh cilantro, chopped
- 1 garlic clove, minced
- 60 milliliters vegetable broth
- Salt and black pepper, to taste
- 60 milliliters black olives, chopped
- 1 teaspoon jerk seasoning

1. Heat the olive oil in a large pot over medium heat. Brown the beef on all sides for 4-5 minutes. Remove from the pot and set aside.
2. Stir-fry the red bell peppers, green chilies, jerk seasoning, garlic, scotch bonnet pepper, onion, ginger paste, and soy sauce in the pot for 5-6 minutes.
3. Add the tomatoes and broth to the pot and bring to a boil. Reduce heat and simmer for 1 hour.
4. Stir in the olives and adjust the seasonings to taste. Serve sprinkled with cilantro.

PER SERVING

Calories:235 | Fat: 13.4g | Net Carbs:2.8g | Protein 25.8g

Shredded Beef with Herbs

Prep time: 5 minutes | Cook time: 50 minutes |Serves 4

- 15 milliliters olive oil
- 450 grams rib eye, cut into strips
- 45 milliliters rice wine
- 120 milliliters beef bone broth
- Sea salt and black pepper, to taste
- 4 tablespoons fresh parsley, finely chopped
- 4 tablespoons fresh chives, finely chopped
- 4 chipotle peppers in adobo sauce, chopped
- 2 garlic cloves, crushed
- 2 small-sized ripe tomatoes, pureed
- 1 yellow onion, peeled and chopped
- 1/2 teaspoon dry mustard
- 1/4 teaspoon dried basil
- 1/4 teaspoon dried marjoram

1. Heat the oil in a large frying pan over a medium-high heat. Sear the beef for 6-7 minutes, stirring periodically. Work in batches.
2. Add the remaining ingredients, reduce the heat to medium-low and simmer for 40 minutes.
3. Shred the beef and serve. Bon appétit!

PER SERVING

Calories: 421 | Fat: 35.7g | Carbs: 5.9g | Fiber: 1g | Protein: 19.7g

Greek Pork with Olives

Prep time: 45 minutes | Cook time: 25 minutes | Serves 4

- 4 bone-in pork chops
- Salt and black pepper, to taste
- 1 teaspoon dried rosemary
- 3 garlic cloves, peeled and minced
- 1/2 cup kalamata olives, pitted and sliced
- 2 tablespoons olive oil
- 1/4 cup vegetable broth

1. Preheat the oven to 220 degrees Celsius (425 degrees Fahrenheit). Season the pork chops with salt and pepper. Place the pork chops in a roasting pan. Stir in the garlic, olives, olive oil, broth, and rosemary.
2. Roast for 10 minutes, then reduce the heat to 175 degrees Celsius (350 degrees Fahrenheit) and roast for an additional 25 minutes, or until the pork chops are cooked through.
3. Slice the pork chops and sprinkle with pan juices. Serve immediately.

PER SERVING

Calories:415 | Fat: 25.2g | Net Carbs: 2.2g | Protein: 36g

Chapter 6

Seafood & Fish Recipes

Grilled Tuna Steaks with Shirataki Pad Thai

Prep time: 30 minutes | Cook time: 5 minutes |Serves 4

- 1 pack (200 grams) shirataki noodles
- 4 cups water
- 1 red bell pepper, sliced
- 4 tablespoons soy sauce, sugar-free
- 2 teaspoons ginger-garlic paste
- 1 teaspoon chili powder
- 1 tablespoon water
- 4 tuna steaks
- Salt and black pepper, to taste
- 1 tablespoon olive oil
- 15 milliliters parsley, chopped

1. Rinse the shirataki noodles under cold running water in a colander. Bring a large pot of salted water to a boil and cook the noodles for 2 minutes. Drain and set aside.
2. Preheat a grill to medium-high heat. Season the tuna steaks with salt, pepper, and olive oil. Grill for 3 minutes per side, or until cooked through.
3. In a bowl, whisk together the soy sauce, ginger-garlic paste, chili powder, water, and olive oil. Add the red bell pepper and noodles and toss to coat.
4. To serve, place the noodles on a serving plate and top with the tuna steaks. Garnish with parsley.

PER SERVING

Calories:287 | Fat: 16.2g | Net Carbs:6.8g | Protein 23.4g

Grilled Salmon with Radish Salad

Prep time: 22 minutes | Cook time: 8 minutes |Serves 4

- 450 g salmon, cut into 4 steaks each
- 1 cup radishes, sliced
- Salt and black pepper, to taste
- 8 green olives, pitted and chopped
- 1 cup arugula
- 2 large tomatoes, diced
- 3 tablespoons red wine vinegar
- 2 green onions, sliced
- 3 tablespoons olive oil
- 2 slices zero-carb bread, cubed
- 15 ml parsley, chopped

1. In a bowl, mix the radishes, olives, black pepper, arugula, tomatoes, red wine vinegar, green onion, olive oil, bread, and parsley. Let sit for the flavors to incorporate.
2. Season the salmon steaks with salt and pepper. Grill on both sides for 8 minutes in total. Serve the salmon on a bed of the radish salad.

PER SERVING

Calories:338 | Fat: 21.7g | Net Carbs:3.1g | Protein 28.5g

Mediterranean Tilapia Bake

Prep time: 30 minutes | Cook time: 23 minutes |Serves 4

- 4 tilapia fillets
- 2 garlic cloves, minced
- 1 teaspoon basil, chopped
- 400 g canned tomatoes
- 1/4 teaspoon chili powder
- 4 tablespoons white wine
- 2 tablespoons olive oil
- 1/2 red onion, chopped
- 2 tablespoons parsley, chopped
- 10 black olives, pitted and halved

1. Preheat oven to 180 degrees Celsius (350 degrees Fahrenheit).
2. Heat the olive oil in a skillet over medium heat and cook the onion and garlic for 3 minutes. Stir in the tomatoes, olives, chili powder, and white wine and bring the mixture to a boil. Reduce heat and simmer for 5 minutes.
3. Place the tilapia fillets in a baking dish and pour over the sauce. Bake in the oven for 10-15 minutes, or until the tilapia is cooked through.
4. Serve garnished with basil.

PER SERVING

Calories:282 | Fat: 15g | Net Carbs:6g | Protein 23g

Bay Shrimp and Ricotta Stuffed Mushrooms

Prep time: 5 minutes | Cook time: 25 minutes |Serves 6

- 15 milliliters butter
- 1/2 cup yellow onion, finely minced
- 2 garlic cloves, minced
- Kosher salt and black pepper, to taste
- 450 grams fresh Bay shrimp, chopped
- 225 grams ricotta cheese, softened
- 30 milliliters mayonnaise
- 450 grams large-sized button mushroom cups
- 150 grams cheddar cheese, shredded

1. Melt the butter in a frying pan over a medium heat. Sauté the onion and garlic for 2-3 minutes, or until just tender and fragrant.
2. Stir in the salt, black pepper, shrimp, ricotta cheese, and mayonnaise. Gently stir to combine well.
3. Preheat the oven to 390 degrees F (200 degrees C).
4. Bake the mushroom cups for 5 minutes, or until they have softened slightly.
5. Spoon the shrimp mixture into each mushroom cup. Return to the oven and bake for 8-11 minutes more. Top each mushroom cup with cheddar cheese.
6. Bake for a further 7 minutes, or until the cheese is melted and bubbly.

PER SERVING

Calories: 354 | Fat: 24.3g | Carbs: 5.3g | Protein: 28g | Fiber: 1.6g

Parmesan Fish Bake

Prep time: 40 minutes | Cook time: 30 to 35 minutes | Serves 4

- 2 salmon fillets, cubed
- 3 white fish fillets, cubed
- 1 head broccoli, cut into florets
- 1 tablespoon melted butter
- Salt and black pepper, to taste
- 1 cup crème fraîche
- 1/4 cup grated Parmesan cheese
- Grated Parmesan cheese, for topping

1. Preheat the oven to 200 degrees Celsius (400 degrees Fahrenheit) and grease an 8 x 8 inch baking dish with cooking spray. Toss the fish cubes and broccoli in butter and season with salt and pepper to taste. Spread in the greased dish.
2. Mix the crème fraîche with Parmesan cheese. Pour and smear the cream on the fish, and sprinkle with some more Parmesan cheese. Bake for 25 to 30 minutes, or until golden brown on top. Let stand for 5 minutes before serving.

PER SERVING

Calories:354 | Fat: 17g | Net Carbs: 4g | Protein: 28g

Baked Haddock with Cheesy Hazelnut Topping

Prep time: 50 minutes | Cook time: 23 minutes |Serves 4

- 2 tablespoons butter
- 1 shallot, sliced
- 450 grams haddock fillet
- 2 hard-boiled eggs, chopped
- 125 milliliters water
- 90 grams hazelnut flour
- 500 milliliters sour cream
- 15 milliliters parsley, chopped
- 75 grams pork rinds, crushed
- 150 grams mozzarella cheese, grated
- Salt and black pepper, to taste

1. Melt the butter in a saucepan over medium heat and sauté the shallots for 3 minutes.
2. Reduce the heat to low and stir in the hazelnut flour to form a roux. Cook the roux for 1-2 minutes, or until golden brown.
3. Stir in the sour cream until the mixture is smooth. Season with salt and pepper, and stir in the parsley.
4. Spread the haddock fillet in a greased baking dish. Sprinkle the eggs on top and spoon the sauce over.
5. In a bowl, mix the pork rinds with the mozzarella cheese. Sprinkle the mixture over the sauce.
6. Bake in the oven for 20 minutes at 190 degrees Celsius (370 degrees Fahrenheit), or until the top is golden and the sauce and cheese are bubbly.

PER SERVING

Calories:788 | Fat: 57g | Net Carbs:8.5g | Protein 65g

Thai-Style Tuna Fillets

Prep time: 5 minutes | Cook time: 25 minutes |Serves 4

- 15 milliliters peanut oil
- 4 tuna fillets
- 1 teaspoon freshly grated ginger
- Kosher salt and black pepper, to taste
- 1/4 teaspoon cayenne pepper
- 1/2 teaspoon cumin seeds
- 1/8 teaspoon ground cinnamon
- 2 scallions, chopped
- 2 garlic cloves, minced
- 1 tablespoon fresh cilantro, chopped
- 1 teaspoon Sriracha sauce
- 4 tablespoons mayonnaise
- 125 milliliters sour cream
- 1 teaspoon stone-ground mustard

1. Preheat the oven to 190 degrees C (375 degrees F). Line a baking sheet with foil.
2. Place the tuna fillets onto the prepared baking sheet and fold up all 4 sides of the foil.
3. Add the peanut oil, grated ginger, salt, black pepper, cayenne pepper, cumin seeds, and cinnamon.
4. Fold the sides of the foil over the fish fillets, sealing the packet. Bake until cooked through, approximately 20 minutes.
5. To make the sauce, whisk together all of the sauce ingredients. Serve immediately and enjoy!

PER SERVING

Calories: 389 | Fat: 17.9g | Carbs: 3.5g | Protein: 50.3g | Fiber: 0.3g

Fish Patties with Creamed Horseradish Sauce

Prep time: 5 minutes | Cook time: 20 minutes |Serves 4

- 450 grams cod fillets
- 2 eggs, beaten
- 1 tablespoon flax seeds meal
- 100 grams parmesan cheese, grated
- 2 tablespoons olive oil
- 4 tablespoons mayonnaise
- 4 tablespoons ricotta cheese
- 1 teaspoon creamed horseradish
- 2 green onions, chopped
- 1 tablespoon fresh basil, chopped

1. Steam the cod fillets until cooked through, approximately 10 minutes. Flake the fish with a fork and add in the beaten eggs, flax seeds meal, and parmesan cheese.
2. Shape the mixture into 4 equal patties. Heat the olive oil in a non-stick frying pan. Fry the fish patties over a medium heat for 3 minutes per side.
3. In the meantime, whisk together the sauce ingredients until everything is well incorporated.
4. Serve the fish patties with the creamed horseradish sauce.

PER SERVING

Calories: 346 | Fat: 23.3g | Carbs: 7g | Protein: 26.3g | Fiber: 0.7g

Sea Bass Medley with Peppers

Prep time: 5 minutes | Cook time: 20 minutes |Serves 6

- 30 milliliters butter, at room temperature
- 1/2 cup leek, chopped
- 1/2 cup bell pepper, chopped
- 1/2 cup serrano pepper, chopped
- 2 garlic cloves, minced
- 2 tablespoons fresh coriander, chopped
- 2 vine-ripe tomatoes, pureed
- 1 liter fish stock
- 900 grams sea bass fillets, chopped into small chunks
- 1 tablespoon Old Bay seasoning
- 1/4 teaspoon sea salt, to taste
- 1 bay leaf

1. Melt the butter in a heavy-bottomed saucepan over a medium heat. Stir in the leek and peppers and sauté for about 5 minutes, or until tender.
2. Stir in the garlic and continue to sauté for 30 to 40 seconds more.
3. Add in the remaining ingredients; gently stir to combine. Reduce the heat to medium-low and partially cover the saucepan.
4. Cook for 10 minutes, or until thoroughly heated. Discard the bay leaf and serve warm.

PER SERVING

Calories: 227 | Fat: 8.3g | Carbs: 4.8g | Protein: 32.3g | Fiber: 0.9g

Skillet Shrimp and Sea Scallop with Scallions

Prep time: 5 minutes | Cook time: 15 minutes |Serves 2

- 15 milliliters olive oil
- 1/4 cup scallions, chopped
- 1 garlic clove, minced
- 125 grams shrimp, peeled and deveined
- 125 grams sea scallops
- 2 tablespoons rum
- 125 milliliters fish broth
- 1/4 teaspoon Cajun seasoning
- Sea salt and black pepper, to taste
- 1 tablespoon fresh parsley, chopped

1. Heat the olive oil in a sauté pan over a medium heat. Sauté the scallions and garlic until just tender and fragrant.
2. Add the shrimp and sea scallops and sear for 2-3 minutes per side, or until they are firm. Add a splash of rum to deglaze the pan.
3. Pour in the fish broth, Cajun seasoning, salt, and pepper. Bring to a simmer and cook for 2-3 minutes, or until the sauce has thickened slightly.
4. Serve warm garnished with fresh parsley.

PER SERVING

Calories: 305 | Fat: 8.8g |Carbs: 2.7g | Protein: 47.3g | Fiber: 0.7g

Lemon Garlic Shrimp

Prep time: 22 minutes | Cook time: 6 minutes |
Serves 6

- 125g butter, divided
- 1kg peeled and deveined shrimp
- Salt and black pepper, to taste
- 1/4 teaspoon sweet paprika
- 1 tablespoon minced garlic
- 45ml water
- 1 lemon, zested and juiced
- 2 tablespoons chopped parsley

1. Melt half of the butter in a large skillet over medium heat. Season the shrimp with salt, pepper, and paprika. Add the shrimp to the butter and stir in the garlic. Cook the shrimp for 4 minutes on both sides, or until pink. Remove to a bowl and set aside.
2. Add the remaining butter to the skillet. Stir in the lemon zest, juice, and water. Add the shrimp, parsley, and adjust the seasoning with salt and pepper. Cook for 2 minutes, or until heated through. Serve the shrimp and sauce with squash pasta.

PER SERVING

Calories:258 | Fat: 22g | Net Carbs: 2g | Protein: 13g

Creamy Herb Monkfish Fillets

Prep time: 5 minutes | Cook time:20 minutes
|Serves 6

- 30 milliliters olive oil
- 6 monkfish fillets
- Sea salt and black pepper, to taste
- 2 green onions, sliced
- 2 green garlic stalks, sliced
- 125 milliliters sour cream
- 1 teaspoon oregano
- 1 teaspoon basil
- 1 teaspoon rosemary
- 100 grams cheddar cheese, shredded
- 2 tablespoons fresh chives, chopped

1. Heat the olive oil in a frying pan over a medium heat. Once hot, sear the monkfish fillets for 3 minutes, or until golden brown. Flip them and cook on the other side for 3-4 minutes more.
2. Season with salt and black pepper. Transfer the monkfish fillets to a lightly greased casserole dish. Add the green onions and green garlic.
3. In a mixing bowl, thoroughly combine the sour cream with the oregano, basil, rosemary, and cheddar cheese.
4. Spoon the mixture into the casserole dish and bake in a preheated oven at 180 degrees C (360 degrees F) for 11 minutes, or until golden brown on top.
5. Garnish with fresh chives and serve.

PER SERVING

Calories: 229 | Fat: 12.5g | Carbs: 2.2g | Protein: 25.9g | Fiber: 0.1g

Summer Salad with Cod Fish

Prep time: 5 minutes | Cook time:15 minutes |Serves 5

- 60 milliliters extra-virgin olive oil
- 5 cod fillets
- 60 milliliters balsamic vinegar
- 1 tablespoon stone-ground mustard
- Sea salt and black pepper, to season
- 225 grams green cabbage, shredded
- 500 grams lettuce, cut into small pieces
- 1 red onion, sliced
- 1 garlic clove, minced
- 1 teaspoon red pepper flakes

1. Heat 1 tablespoon of the olive oil in a large frying pan over a medium heat.
2. Once hot, fry the fish fillets for 5 minutes, or until golden brown. Flip them and cook on the other side for 4-5 minutes more, working in batches to avoid overcrowding the pan.
3. Flake the cod fillets with two forks and reserve.
4. To make the dressing, whisk together the remaining tablespoon of olive oil, balsamic vinegar, mustard, salt, and black pepper.
5. Combine the green cabbage, lettuce, onion, and garlic in a salad bowl. Dress the salad and top with the reserved fish.
6. Garnish with red pepper flakes and serve.

PER SERVING

Calories: 276 | Fat: 6.9g | Carbs: 6.4g | Protein: 42.7g | Fiber: 1.7g

Traditional Fish Curry

Prep time: 5 minutes | Cook time:20 minutes | Serving 4

- 15 milliliters peanut oil
- 3 green cardamom pods
- 1 teaspoon cumin seeds
- 1/2 cup shallot, chopped
- 1/2 cup red chili pepper, chopped
- 1/2 cup red bell pepper, chopped
- 1 teaspoon ginger-garlic paste
- 250 milliliters tomato puree
- 250 milliliters chicken broth
- 1 tablespoon curry paste
- 750 grams tilapia
- 1 cinnamon stick
- Sea salt and black pepper, to taste

1. Heat the peanut oil in a saucepan over a medium heat. Toast the cardamom pods and cumin seeds for 2 minutes, or until aromatic.
2. Add in the shallot, red chili, and bell pepper and sauté for 2 minutes more, or until just tender and translucent.
3. Add in the ginger-garlic paste and sauté for an additional 30 seconds. Pour in the tomato puree and chicken broth. Bring to a boil.
4. Reduce the heat to medium-low and stir in the curry paste, tilapia, cinnamon, salt, and black pepper. Simmer, partially covered, for 10 minutes more.
5. Flake the fish and serve in individual bowls.

PER SERVING

Calories: 209 | Fat: 6.5g | Carbs: 3.1g | Protein: 34.8g | Fiber: 0.8g

Chapter 7

Side Dishes & Snacks

Stuffed Peppers with Cauliflower and Cheese

Prep time: 5 minutes | Cook time: 45 minutes |Serves 6

- 2 tablespoons vegetable oil
- 2 tablespoons onion, chopped
- 1 clove garlic, crushed
- 225 grams ground pork
- 225 grams ground turkey
- 250 grams cauliflower rice
- 1/2 teaspoon salt
- 1/4 teaspoon crushed red pepper flakes
- 1/2 teaspoon black pepper
- 1 teaspoon dried parsley flakes
- 6 medium-sized bell peppers, deseeded and halved
- 125 milliliters tomato sauce
- 100 grams Cheddar cheese, grated

1. Heat the oil in a frying pan over a medium heat. Once hot, sauté the onion and garlic for 2-3 minutes, or until softened.
2. Add the ground meat and cook for 6 minutes, or until browned. Stir in the cauliflower rice and seasonings, and cook for a further 3 minutes.
3. Divide the filling between the prepared bell peppers. Cover with a piece of foil. Place the peppers in a baking dish and pour over the tomato sauce.
4. Bake in a preheated oven at 190 degrees Celsius for 20 minutes. Remove the foil, top with the cheese, and bake for a further 10 minutes, or until the cheese is melted and golden brown.

PER SERVING

Calories: 244 | Fat: 12.9g | Carbs: 3.2g | Fiber: 1g | Protein: 16.5g

The Best Zucchini Fritters Ever

Prep time: 5 minutes | Cook time: 40 minutes |Serves 6

- 450 grams zucchini, grated and drained
- 1 egg
- 1 teaspoon chopped fresh Italian parsley
- 75 grams almond meal
- 100 grams goat cheese, crumbled
- Salt and black pepper, to taste
- 1/4 teaspoon crushed red pepper flakes
- 1 tablespoon olive oil

1. In a large bowl, combine all the ingredients except for the olive oil.
2. Cover the bowl and refrigerate for 30 minutes.
3. Heat the olive oil in a non-stick frying pan over a medium heat.
4. Scoop heaped tablespoons of the zucchini mixture into the hot oil and cook for 3-4 minutes on each side, or until golden brown.
5. Transfer the fritters to a paper towel to drain any excess oil.
6. Serve immediately and enjoy!

PER SERVING

Calories: 111 | Fat: 8.9g | Carbs: 3.2g | Fiber: 1g | Protein: 5.8g

German Fried Cabbage

Prep time: 5 minutes | Cook time: 20 minutes |Serves 3

- 115 grams bacon, diced
- 1 medium onion, chopped
- 2 garlic cloves, crushed
- 1/2 teaspoon caraway seeds
- 1 bay leaf
- 1/2 teaspoon cayenne pepper
- 450 grams red cabbage, shredded
- 1/4 teaspoon black pepper, to taste
- 250 milliliters beef bone broth

1. Heat a non-stick frying pan over a medium heat. Cook the bacon for 3-4 minutes, stirring continuously, then set aside.
2. In the same pan, sauté the onion for 2-3 minutes, or until softened. Add the garlic and caraway seeds and cook for 30 seconds, or until fragrant.
3. Add the remaining ingredients and stir to combine. Reduce the heat to low, cover, and cook for 10 minutes, stirring occasionally, or until the cabbage is tender.
4. Serve in individual bowls, garnished with the reserved bacon. Enjoy!

PER SERVING

Calories: 243 | Fat: 22.2g | Carbs: 6.8g | Protein: 6.5g | Fiber: 1.9g

Spicy Glazed Aubergine

Prep time: 5 minutes | Cook time: 20 minutes |Serves 4

- 1 teaspoon dried basil
- 1/2 teaspoon dried oregano
- 1/2 teaspoon dried rosemary
- 1/2 teaspoon sea salt
- 1 large aubergine, sliced lengthways
- 2 tablespoons coconut aminos
- 1 teaspoon balsamic vinegar
- 1 tablespoon olive oil
- 1/2 teaspoon Sriracha sauce
- 1/4 cup fresh chives, chopped

1. Preheat the oven to 218 degrees Celsius.
2. In a bowl, combine the basil, oregano, rosemary, and salt. Toss the aubergine slices in the herb mixture.
3. Place the aubergine slices on a parchment-lined baking tray. Roast in the preheated oven for 15 minutes.
4. Meanwhile, in a small bowl, whisk together the coconut aminos, vinegar, olive oil, and Sriracha sauce.
5. Drizzle the Sriracha mixture over the aubergine slices.
6. Place the baking tray under the preheated grill for 3-5 minutes, or until the aubergine is glazed and slightly charred.
7. Garnish with fresh chives and serve warm.

PER SERVING

Calories: 102 |Fat: 7g | Carbs: 8g | Protein: 1.6g | Fiber: 4.7g

Italian-Style Stuffed Peppers

Prep time: 5 minutes | Cook time: 30 minutes |Serves 4

- 1 tablespoon vegetable oil
- 1 garlic clove, crushed
- 1/2 cup celery, finely chopped
- 1/2 onion, finely chopped
- 115 grams ground pork
- Salt, to taste
- 1 teaspoon Italian seasoning
- 2 sweet Italian peppers, deseeded and halved
- 1 large tomato, pureed
- 100 grams cheddar cheese, grated

1. Heat the vegetable oil in a frying pan over a medium heat. Sauté the garlic, celery, and onion until softened.
2. Stir in the ground pork and cook for 3 minutes, or until browned. Season with salt and Italian seasoning. Divide the filling between the pepper halves.
3. Pour the pureed tomato into a lightly greased baking dish. Place the stuffed peppers in the baking dish.
4. Bake in a preheated oven at 199 degrees Celsius for 20 minutes. Sprinkle with the cheddar cheese and bake for an additional 4-6 minutes, or until the cheese is melted and golden brown. Serve warm and enjoy!

PER SERVING

Calories: 313 | Fat: 21.3g | Carbs: 5.7g | Protein: 20.2g | Fiber: 1.9g

Butternut Squash and Spinach Stew

Prep time: 5 minutes | Cook time: 35 minutes |Serves 4

- 2 tablespoons olive oil
- 1 onion, peeled and diced
- 1 garlic clove, crushed
- 225 grams butternut squash, diced
- 1 celery stalk, chopped
- 750 milliliters vegetable broth
- Salt and black pepper, to taste
- 4 cups baby spinach
- 4 tablespoons sour cream

1. Heat the olive oil in a large saucepan over a medium heat. Sauté the onion until soft and translucent.
2. Add the garlic and cook for 30 seconds, or until fragrant.
3. Stir in the butternut squash, celery, broth, salt, and pepper. Bring to a boil, then reduce the heat to low and simmer for 30 minutes, or until the butternut squash is tender.
4. Stir in the baby spinach and cover with the lid. Let the spinach wilt in the residual heat for a few minutes.
5. Serve immediately, dolloped with sour cream.

PER SERVING

Calories: 148 | Fat: 11.5g | Carbs: 6.8g | Protein: 2.5g | Fiber: 2.3g

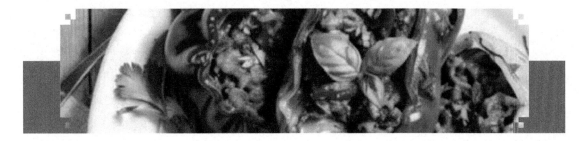

Sausage Stuffed Romaine Boats

Prep time: 5 minutes | Cook time: 15 minutes |Serves 4

- 225 grams pork sausage, sliced
- 1 green bell pepper, deseeded and chopped
- 1 garlic clove, crushed
- 125 milliliters tomato puree
- 1/4 teaspoon black pepper
- 1/2 teaspoon fennel seeds
- Himalayan salt, to taste
- 1 head romaine lettuce, leaves separated
- 2 spring onions, chopped

1. Heat a non-stick frying pan over a medium heat. Cook the sausage for 5-7 minutes, or until browned, breaking it up with a fork as it cooks.
2. Stir in the bell pepper and garlic and cook for 2-3 minutes, or until softened.
3. Add the tomato puree, black pepper, fennel seeds, and salt. Stir to combine and cook for 1 minute more.
4. Arrange the lettuce leaves on a serving platter. Top each leaf with the sausage mixture and garnish with spring onions. Serve immediately.

PER SERVING

Calories: 230 | Fat: 18.1g | Carbs: 5.6g | Protein: 10.2g | Fiber: 2.1g

Zoodles with Romano Cheese and Mushroom Sauce

Prep time: 5 minutes | Cook time: 15 minutes |Serves 3

- 2 tablespoons olive oil
- 450 grams button mushrooms, chopped
- 2 garlic cloves, crushed
- 250 milliliters tomato puree
- 450 grams zucchini, spiralized
- Salt and black pepper, to taste
- 75 grams Pecorino Romano cheese, freshly grated

1. Heat the olive oil in a large saucepan over a medium heat. Cook the mushrooms for 4-5 minutes, or until softened and fragrant.
2. Stir in the garlic and cook for 30 seconds, or until fragrant.
3. Add the tomato puree and zucchini. Reduce the heat to low, partially cover, and cook for 6 minutes, or until the zucchini is tender.
4. Season with salt and pepper to taste.
5. Divide the zoodles and sauce between serving plates. Top with Pecorino Romano cheese and serve warm.

PER SERVING

Calories: 160 | Fat: 10.6g | Carbs: 7.4g | Protein: 10g | Fiber: 3.4g

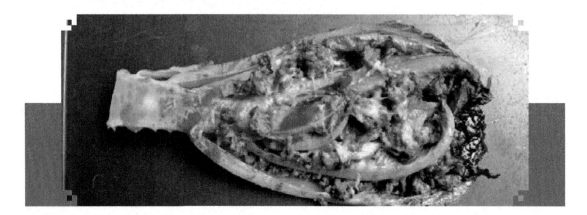

Oven-Baked Cheesy Zucchini Rounds

Prep time: 5 minutes | Cook time: 20 minutes |Serves 6

- 30 milliliters olive oil
- 2 eggs
- 1/2 teaspoon smoked paprika
- Sea salt and black pepper, to taste
- 900 grams zucchini, sliced into rounds
- 100 grams Romano cheese, grated

1. Preheat the oven to 220 degrees C (420 degrees F). Line a baking sheet with parchment paper.
2. In a mixing bowl, whisk together the olive oil, eggs, paprika, salt, and pepper. Dip the zucchini slices in the egg mixture.
3. Top with the grated Romano cheese.
4. Arrange the zucchini rounds on the baking sheet and bake for 15 minutes, or until golden brown. Serve at room temperature.

PER SERVING

Calories: 137 | Fat: 9.8g | Carbs: 5.7g | Protein: 8.8g | Fiber: 1.8g

Zucchini Gratin with Feta Cheese

Prep time: 65 minutes | Cook time: 30 to 40 minutes | Serves 6

- 2 pounds zucchini, sliced
- 2 red bell peppers, seeded and sliced
- Salt and black pepper, to taste
- 1.5 cups crumbled feta cheese
- 2 tablespoons butter, melted
- 1/4 teaspoon xanthan gum
- 1/2 cup heavy whipping cream

1. Preheat the oven to 190 degrees Celsius (370 degrees Fahrenheit). Place the sliced zucchini in a colander over the sink, sprinkle with salt, and let sit for 20 minutes. Transfer to paper towels to drain the excess liquid.
2. Grease a baking dish with cooking spray and make a layer of zucchini and bell peppers overlapping one another. Season with pepper, and sprinkle with feta cheese. Repeat the layering process a second time.
3. Combine the butter, xanthan gum, and whipping cream in a bowl, stir to mix completely, and pour over the vegetables. Bake for 30-40 minutes, or until golden brown on top.

PER SERVING

Calories:264 | Fat: 21g | Net Carbs: 4g | Protein: 14g

Deviled Eggs with Mustard and Chives

Prep time: **5 minutes** | Cook time: **20 minutes** |Serves 10

- 8 eggs
- 30 milliliters cream cheese
- 1 teaspoon Dijon mustard
- 15 milliliters mayonnaise
- 15 milliliters tomato puree, no sugar added
- 5 milliliters balsamic vinegar
- Sea salt and black pepper, to taste
- 1/4 teaspoon cayenne pepper
- 2 tablespoons chives, chopped

1. Place the eggs in a single layer in a saucepan. Add water to cover the eggs and bring to a boil.
2. Cover, turn off the heat, and let the eggs stand for 15 minutes. Drain the eggs and peel them under cold running water.
3. Slice the eggs in half lengthwise; remove the yolks and thoroughly combine with cream cheese, mustard, mayo, tomato puree, vinegar, salt, black pepper, and cayenne pepper.
4. Divide the yolk mixture among the egg whites. Garnish with fresh chives and enjoy!

PER SERVING

Calories: 149 | Fat: 11.3g | Carbs: 1.6g | Fiber: 0.1g | Protein: 9.4g

Cheesy Stuffed Jalapeños

Prep time: **5 minutes** | Cook time: **35 minutes** |Serves 10

- 50 grams bacon, chopped
- 225 grams ground pork
- 225 grams ground beef
- 1/2 cup red onion, chopped
- 2 garlic cloves, minced
- 1 teaspoon taco seasoning mix
- Sea salt and black pepper, to taste
- 1/2 cup tomato puree
- 1 teaspoon stone-ground mustard
- 20 jalapeño peppers, halved lengthwise and deseeded
- 100 grams Parmesan cheese, grated

1. Preheat the oven to 190 degrees C (390 degrees F).
2. Heat a non-stick frying pan over a medium-high heat. Cook the bacon, pork, and beef for 4 minutes, or until no longer pink.
3. Add the onion and garlic and cook for an additional 3 minutes, or until tender. Season with taco seasoning mix, salt, and black pepper. Stir in the tomato puree and mustard.
4. Continue to cook over medium-low heat for 4 minutes more. Spoon the mixture into the jalapeño halves.
5. Bake in the preheated oven for 20 minutes, or until heated through. Sprinkle with Parmesan cheese and bake for an additional 6 minutes, or until the cheese is golden brown.

PER SERVING

Calories: 189 | Fat: 13.2g | Carbs: 4.9g | Protein: 12.7g | Fiber: 1.1g

Easy Caprese Appetizer

Prep time: 5 minutes | Cook time: 10 minutes |Serves 10

- 2 tablespoons extra-virgin olive oil
- 2 tablespoons balsamic vinegar
- 1 tablespoon mixed dried herbs (such as oregano, thyme, and basil)
- 8 slices Parma ham (prosciutto can be used as an alternative)
- 8 slices Salami (soppressata can be used as an alternative)
- 16 cherry tomatoes
- 8 black olives, pitted
- 225g mozzarella, cubed
- 2 tablespoons fresh basil leaves, chopped
- 1 red bell pepper, sliced
- 1 yellow bell pepper, sliced
- Pinch of coarse sea salt, to taste

1. In a small mixing bowl, prepare the vinaigrette by whisking the olive oil, balsamic vinegar, and mixed dried herbs. Set aside.
2. Assemble the ingredients on wooden or metal skewers.
3. Arrange the skewers on a serving platter. Season with a pinch of coarse sea salt to taste. Serve the vinaigrette on the side, and enjoy!

PER SERVING

Calories: 141 | Fat: 8.2g | Carbs: 3.3g | Protein: 12.9g | Fiber: 1g

Bacon-Wrapped Stuffed Poblanos

Prep time: 5 minutes | Cook time: 35 minutes |Serves 16

- 280g curd cheese (cottage cheese)
- 170g grated Swiss cheese
- Sea salt and ground black pepper, to taste
- 1/2 teaspoon shallot powder
- 1/2 teaspoon ground cumin
- 1/3 teaspoon mustard seeds
- 8 large poblano peppers, deveined and halved
- 16 rashers of streaky bacon, sliced lengthwise

1. In a mixing bowl, combine the curd cheese, salt, black pepper, shallot powder, ground cumin, and mustard seeds until well combined.
2. Divide the cheese mixture between the halved pepper halves. Wrap each pepper with 2 slices of bacon and secure with toothpicks.
3. Arrange the stuffed peppers on a baking sheet with a wire rack.
4. Bake in the preheated oven at 200 degrees Celsius (390 degrees F) for about 30 minutes until the bacon is sizzling and browned. Bon appétit!

PER SERVING

Calories: 183 | Fat: 14g | Carbs: 5.9g | Protein: 9g | Fiber: 0.7g

Chapter 8

Desserts & Drink

Lassi with Lychee, Yogurt and Milk

Prep time: 2 hours 28 minutes | Cook time: 20 minutes |Serves 4

- 500 grams lychee pulp, seeded
- 625 milliliters coconut milk
- 16 grams xylitol
- 2 limes, zested and juiced
- 375 milliliters plain yogurt
- 1 lemongrass stalk, white part only, crushed
- Toasted coconut shavings, for garnish

1. In a saucepan, combine the lychee pulp, coconut milk, xylitol, lemongrass, and lime zest. Bring to a boil over medium heat, stirring constantly, for 3 minutes. Reduce the heat to low and simmer for 1 minute. Remove from the heat and let the mixture sit for 15 minutes.
2. Discard the lemongrass. Pour the mixture into a blender and add the yogurt and lime juice. Blend until smooth, about 1 minute. Pour into a jug and refrigerate for 2 hours, or until cold. Stir before serving. Garnish with toasted coconut shavings.

PER SERVING

Calories:283 | Fat: 23.6g | Net Carbs:3.2g | Protein 6g

Blackcurrant Juice with Lime

Prep time: 8 minutes | Cook time: 4 minutes |Serves 4

- 5 unflavored tea bags
- 500 milliliters water
- 125 milliliters sugar-free blackcurrant extract
- 15 milliliters erythritol
- Ice cubes, for serving
- Lime slices, to garnish

1. In a saucepan over medium heat, bring the water to a boil for 4 minutes. Stir in the erythritol to dissolve, then remove from the heat. Steep the tea bags in the water for 3 minutes.
2. Remove the tea bags and let the tea cool down. Add in the blackcurrant extract and stir until well combined.
3. Pour the ice cubes into a pitcher and place it in the fridge. Once the tea has cooled down, pour it over the ice cubes in the pitcher.
4. Allow to cool for 3 minutes, then pour the mixture into tall glasses. Add some more ice cubes to each glass and garnish with lime slices. Serve cold.

PER SERVING

Calories:21 | Fat: 0.4g | Net Carbs:2.8g | Protein 0.5g

Lavender and Raspberry Pie

Prep time: 2 hours 25 minutes | Cook time: 30 minutes |Serves 4

- 1 large low-carb pie crust
- 375 milliliters heavy cream
- 40 grams erythritol
- 1 tablespoon culinary lavender
- 1 vanilla bean, seeds scraped
- 2 cups fresh raspberries

1. Preheat the oven to 190 degrees Celsius (380 degrees Fahrenheit). Place the pie crust in a pie dish and bake for 30 minutes, or until golden brown. Remove from the oven and let cool.
2. In a saucepan over medium heat, combine the heavy cream and lavender. Bring to a boil, then remove from the heat and let cool for 1 hour.
3. Strain the cream through a colander to remove the lavender pieces. In a bowl, whisk together the erythritol, vanilla seeds, and strained cream. Pour the mixture into the cooled pie crust.
4. Scatter the raspberries on top of the cream mixture. Refrigerate the pie for 45 minutes, or until set.
5. Serve the pie chilled, topped with additional erythritol.

PER SERVING

Calories:323 | Fat: 33.6g | Net Carbs:11.3g | Protein 5.2g

Lazy Strawberry Mini Cakes

Prep time: 45 minutes | Cook time:40 minutes |Serves 4

- 4 eggs
- 40 grams coconut oil, melted
- 2 cups strawberries, hulled and sliced
- 1 cup coconut milk
- 1 cup almond flour
- 60 grams xylitol
- 1/2 teaspoon vanilla powder
- 1/4 teaspoon powdered sugar
- A pinch of salt

1. Place all ingredients, except coconut oil, berries, and powdered sugar, in a blender and pulse until smooth. Fold in strawberries.
2. Preheat oven to 165 degrees Celsius (330 degrees Fahrenheit). Grease a baking dish with oil.
3. Pour the mixture into the prepared baking dish and bake for 40 minutes, or until a toothpick inserted into the center comes out clean.
4. Let the cakes cool in the pan for 10 minutes, then remove and let cool completely on a wire rack.
5. Sprinkle with powdered sugar and cut into mini cakes. Serve immediately.

PER SERVING

Calories:311 | Fat: 28.3g | Net Carbs:6.4g | Protein 13.7g

Chocolate Cupcakes

Prep time: 45 minutes | Cook time: 5 minutes |Serves 4

- 1 cup almond flour
- 60 grams stevia
- 60 grams unsweetened cocoa powder
- 1 teaspoon baking powder
- 1 large egg
- 125 milliliters plain yogurt
- 40 grams butter, melted
- 85 grams unsweetened dark chocolate chips

1. Preheat the oven to 175 degrees Celsius (350 degrees Fahrenheit). Line a 12-cup muffin tin with paper liners.
2. In a medium bowl, whisk together the almond flour, stevia, cocoa powder, and baking powder.
3. In a separate bowl, whisk together the egg, yogurt, and butter. Gradually add the wet ingredients to the dry ingredients, mixing until just combined. Do not overmix.
4. Fold in the chocolate chips. Fill the prepared muffin cups 3/4 full with batter. Sprinkle with the remaining chocolate chips.
5. Bake for 20 minutes, or until a toothpick inserted into the center comes out clean. Let the cupcakes cool in the tin for 15 minutes before removing to a wire rack to cool completely.

PER SERVING

Calories:210 | Fat: 13g | Net Carbs:3.2g | Protein 3.9g

Lemon Cheesecake with Raspberry

Prep time: 4 hours and 50 minutes | Cook time: 25 minutes | Serves 12

CRUST:

- 2 egg whites
- 60 grams erythritol
- 750 grams desiccated coconut
- 1 teaspoon coconut oil
- 60 grams butter, melted

FILLING:

- 90 milliliters lemon juice
- 170 grams raspberries
- 600 grams erythritol
- 250 milliliters heavy cream
- Zest of 1 lemon
- 90 milliliters lemon juice
- 680 grams cream cheese

1. Preheat the oven to 175 degrees Celsius (350 degrees Fahrenheit). Grease and line the bottom of a springform pan with parchment paper.
2. In a bowl, combine the crust ingredients and mix until well combined. Press the mixture into the prepared springform pan and bake for 25 minutes, or until golden brown. Let cool completely.
3. In a bowl, beat the cream cheese until soft. Add the lemon juice, zest, and erythritol and beat until well combined. In a separate bowl, beat the heavy cream until soft peaks form. Fold the whipped cream into the cream cheese mixture. Gently fold in the raspberries.
4. Pour the filling into the cooled crust and refrigerate for at least 4 hours, or overnight.
5. Serve chilled.

PER SERVING

Calories:215 | Net Carbs:3 g | Fat: 25 g | Protein 5 g

Old-Fashioned Molten Chocolate Cake

Prep time: 5 minutes | Cook time: 15 minutes |Serves 4

- 2 tablespoons coconut flour
- 4 tablespoons cocoa powder, unsweetened
- 1/2 teaspoon baking powder
- 3 medium eggs
- 42g butter, melted
- 42g double cream
- A pinch of Himalayan salt
- 1/4 teaspoon cardamom
- 1/2 teaspoon ground cinnamon
- 1/2 teaspoon rum extract
- 1/2 teaspoon vanilla extract
- 6 tablespoons xylitol (or any preferred sugar substitute)

1. Thoroughly combine the coconut flour, cocoa powder, and baking powder in a mixing bowl.
2. In another mixing bowl, whisk the eggs with the melted butter and double cream; fold this wet mixture into the dry mixture.
3. Add in the remaining ingredients; mix until everything is well blended. Grease 4 ceramic ramekins with nonstick cooking spray; pour the batter into the prepared ramekins.
4. Bake in the preheated oven at 180 degrees Celsius (355 degrees F) for 10 minutes or until the edges have set but the middle is still soft.
5. Carefully lift each chocolate pudding onto a serving plate with a spatula. Bon appétit!

PER SERVING

Calories: 168| Fat: 15.8g | Carbs: 6g | Protein: 4.5g | Fiber: 2.5g

Greek-Style Cheesecake

Prep time: 5 minutes | Cook time: 1 hour 35 minutes |Serves 6

- 240g ground almonds (almond meal)
- 85g butter, melted
- 1/2 teaspoon ground cinnamon
- 2 tablespoons Greek yogurt (Greek-style yogurt)
- 280g cream cheese, softened
- 240g icing sugar substitute (confectioner's Swerve)
- 2 medium eggs

1. Mix the ground almonds, melted butter, and ground cinnamon until well blended. Press the mixture into a parchment-lined baking pan.
2. Then, whip the Greek yogurt, cream cheese, and icing sugar substitute until well combined. Fold in the eggs, one at a time, and mix well after each addition.
3. Pour the filling over the crust in the baking pan. Bake in the preheated oven at 165 degrees Celsius (330 degrees F) for about 30 minutes.
4. Run a sharp paring knife between the cheesecake and the baking pan and allow it to sit on the counter for 1 hour.
5. Cover loosely with plastic wrap and refrigerate overnight. Serve well-chilled and enjoy!

PER SERVING

Calories: 471 | Fat: 45g | Carbs: 6.9g | Protein: 11.5g | Fiber: 4g

Ranch Chicken Wings

Prep time: 5 minutes | Cook time: 55 minutes |Serves 6

- 900 grams chicken wings, patted dry
- Non-stick cooking spray
- Sea salt and cayenne pepper, to taste
- Ranch Dressing:
- 60 milliliters sour cream
- 60 milliliters buttermilk
- 125 milliliters mayonnaise
- 15 milliliters lemon juice
- 1 tablespoon fresh parsley, chopped
- 1 garlic clove, minced
- 4 tablespoons onion, finely chopped
- 1/4 teaspoon dry mustard
- Sea salt and black pepper, to taste

1. Preheat the oven to 220 degrees C (420 degrees F).
2. Spray the chicken wings with cooking spray. Sprinkle the chicken wings with salt and cayenne pepper. Arrange the chicken wings on a parchment-lined baking tray. Bake in the preheated oven for 50 minutes, or until the wings are golden and crispy.
3. Meanwhile, make the dressing by mixing all of the ingredients together. Serve with warm wings.

PER SERVING

Calories: 466 | Fat: 37.2g | Carbs: 1.9g | Fiber: 0.1g | Protein: 28.6g

Puffy Anise Cookies

Prep time: 5 minutes | Cook time: 25 minutes |Serves 10

- 2 tablespoons coconut oil
- 1 tablespoon coconut milk
- 1 medium egg, whisked
- 120g coconut flour
- 120g almond flour
- 1 teaspoon baking powder
- 30g powdered erythritol (or any preferred sugar substitute)
- 1 teaspoon pure anise extract
- 1/4 teaspoon ground cloves
- 1/2 teaspoon ground cinnamon
- A pinch of salt

1. In a mixing bowl, beat the coconut oil, coconut milk, and egg together. In a separate bowl, mix the coconut flour, almond flour, baking powder, powdered erythritol, anise extract, ground cloves, cinnamon, and salt.
2. Add the dry mixture to the wet mixture and mix to combine well. Shape the mixture into small balls and arrange them on a parchment-lined baking pan.
3. Bake in the preheated oven at 180 degrees Celsius (360 degrees F) for about 13 minutes. Transfer the biscuits to cooling racks and let them cool for 10 minutes before serving. Bon appétit!

PER SERVING

Calories: 142 | Fat: 13g | Carbs: 5.2g | Protein: 3.5g | Fiber: 2.4g

Simple Nutty Crepes

Prep time: 5 minutes | Cook time: 15 minutes |Serves 6

- 2 tablespoons ground flaxseed (flaxseed meal)
- 120g almond meal
- 60g fine ground pecans
- 1/2 teaspoon baking powder
- 1/4 teaspoon sea salt
- 4 medium eggs
- 170g ricotta cheese, at room temperature
- 60g pumpkin puree, sugar-free
- 2 tablespoons powdered erythritol (or any preferred sugar substitute)
- 1/2 teaspoon vanilla extract

1. Mix the ground flaxseed, almond meal, fine ground pecans, baking powder, and sea salt in a bowl.
2. Then, gradually fold in the remaining ingredients in the order listed above. Mix on low speed after each addition.
3. Preheat a lightly greased pancake pan or griddle, and cook your pancakes for 2 to 3 minutes per side. Repeat until you run out of batter.
4. Serve the nutty pancakes with heavy cream, icing sugar substitute (confectioner's Swerve), or fresh blackberries if desired. Bon appétit!

PER SERVING

Calories: 260 | Fat: 21.7g | Carbs: 6.9g | Protein: 11.6g | Fiber: 3.8g

Traditional Spanish Frisuelos

Prep time: 5 minutes | Cook time: 20 minutes |Serves 6

- 3 medium eggs
- 1/2 teaspoon maple flavoring (maple extract)
- 60ml double cream
- 115g mascarpone cheese
- A pinch of salt
- A pinch of ground cloves
- 1 tablespoon brandy (cognac)
- 1 teaspoon grated lemon zest
- 1 tablespoon melted butter
- 6 tablespoons icing sugar substitute (confectioners' Swerve)

1. Beat the eggs with the maple flavoring until light and frothy. Fold in the double cream and mascarpone cheese. Mix again until well combined.
2. Stir in the salt, ground cloves, brandy, and grated lemon zest. Mix again until smooth and there aren't any lumps.
3. Coat a frying pan with melted butter using a paper towel. Add a small amount of batter to the hot pan and spread it out to cover the bottom, creating a thin pancake.
4. Cook for about 2 minutes on each side until the pancakes are golden. Transfer your crepe pancake to a large plate and sprinkle icing sugar substitute on top. Repeat until you run out of batter. Enjoy!

PER SERVING

Calories: 137 | Fat: 12.3g | Carbs: 3.2g | Protein: 4.1g | Fiber: 0g

Granny Smith Apple Tart

Prep time: 65 minutes | Cook time: 51 minutes | Serves 8

- 6 tablespoons butter, softened
- 2 cups ground almonds
- 1 teaspoon ground cinnamon
- 75g granulated sweetener
- Filling:
- 1 cup sliced Granny Smith apples
- 50g butter, melted
- 50g granulated sweetener
- 1/2 teaspoon ground cinnamon
- 1/2 teaspoon lemon juice
- Topping:
- 1/4 teaspoon ground cinnamon
- 1 tablespoon granulated sweetener

1. Preheat the oven to 190 degrees Celsius (370 degrees Fahrenheit).
2. In a bowl, combine the butter, almond flour, cinnamon, and sweetener. Press the mixture into the bottom of a greased 9-inch tart pan. Bake for 5 minutes.
3. In a bowl, combine the apples, lemon juice, butter, sweetener, and cinnamon. Pour the mixture over the crust.
4. Bake for 30 minutes, or until the apples are tender. Press the apples down with a spatula, return to the oven, and bake for 20 more minutes, or until the topping is golden brown.
5. In a small bowl, combine the cinnamon and sweetener. Sprinkle over the tart.

PER SERVING

Calories:302 | Fat: 26g | Net Carbs: 6.7g | Protein: 7g

Raspberry Nut Truffles

Prep time: 6 minutes + cooling time | Serves 4

- 2 cups raw cashews
- 2 tablespoons ground flaxseed
- 1 1/2 cups sugar-free raspberry preserves
- 75g granulated sweetener
- 10 ounces unsweetened chocolate chips
- 3 tablespoons olive oil

1. Line a baking sheet with parchment paper and set aside. Blend the cashews and flaxseeds in a food processor for 45 seconds until finely ground; add the raspberry preserves and 50g of the sweetener.
2. Process further for 1 minute until well combined. Form 1-inch balls of the mixture, place on the baking sheet, and freeze for 1 hour or until firmed up.
3. Melt the chocolate chips, oil, and the remaining 25g of sweetener in a microwave for 1 1/2 minutes. Toss the truffles to coat in the chocolate mixture, put on the baking sheet, and freeze further for at least 2 hours.

PER SERVING

Calories:251 | Fat: 18.3g | Net Carbs: 3.5g | Protein: 12g

Appendix 1 Measurement Conversion Chart

Volume Equivalents (Dry)	
US STANDARD	METRIC (APPROXIMATE)
1/8 teaspoon	0.5 mL
1/4 teaspoon	1 mL
1/2 teaspoon	2 mL
3/4 teaspoon	4 mL
1 teaspoon	5 mL
1 tablespoon	15 mL
1/4 cup	59 mL
1/2 cup	118 mL
3/4 cup	177 mL
1 cup	235 mL
2 cups	475 mL
3 cups	700 mL
4 cups	1 L

Volume Equivalents (Liquid)		
US STANDARD	US STANDARD (OUNCES)	METRIC (APPROXIMATE)
2 tablespoons	1 fl.oz.	30 mL
1/4 cup	2 fl.oz.	60 mL
1/2 cup	4 fl.oz.	120 mL
1 cup	8 fl.oz.	240 mL
1 1/2 cup	12 fl.oz.	355 mL
2 cups or 1 pint	16 fl.oz.	475 mL
4 cups or 1 quart	32 fl.oz.	1 L
1 gallon	128 fl.oz.	4 L

Temperatures Equivalents	
FAHRENHEIT(F)	CELSIUS(C) APPROXIMATE)
225 °F	107 °C
250 °F	120 ° °C
275 °F	135 °C
300 °F	150 °C
325 °F	160 °C
350 °F	180 °C
375 °F	190 °C
400 °F	205 °C
425 °F	220 °C
450 °F	235 °C
475 °F	245 °C
500 °F	260 °C

Weight Equivalents	
US STANDARD	METRIC (APPROXIMATE)
1 ounce	28 g
2 ounces	57 g
5 ounces	142 g
10 ounces	284 g
15 ounces	425 g
16 ounces (1 pound)	455 g
1.5 pounds	680 g
2 pounds	907 g

Appendix 2 The Dirty Dozen and Clean Fifteen

The Environmental Working Group (EWG) is a nonprofit, nonpartisan organization dedicated to protecting human health and the environment Its mission is to empower people to live healthier lives in a healthier environment. This organization publishes an annual list of the twelve kinds of produce, in sequence, that have the highest amount of pesticide residue-the Dirty Dozen-as well as a list of the fifteen kinds ofproduce that have the least amount of pesticide residue-the Clean Fifteen.

THE DIRTY DOZEN

The 2016 Dirty Dozen includes the following produce. These are considered among the year's most important produce to buy organic:

Strawberries	Spinach
Apples	Tomatoes
Nectarines	Bell peppers
Peaches	Cherry tomatoes
Celery	Cucumbers
Grapes	Kale/collard greens
Cherries	Hot peppers

The Dirty Dozen list contains two additional itemskale/collard greens and hot peppers-because they tend to contain trace levels of highly hazardous pesticides.

THE CLEAN FIFTEEN

The least critical to buy organically are the Clean Fifteen list. The following are on the 2016 list:

Avocados	Papayas
Corn	Kiw
Pineapples	Eggplant
Cabbage	Honeydew
Sweet peas	Grapefruit
Onions	Cantaloupe
Asparagus	Cauliflower
Mangos	

Some of the sweet corn sold in the United States are made from genetically engineered (GE) seedstock. Buy organic varieties of these crops to avoid GE produce.

Appendix 3 Index

Kimberly T. Frank

Printed in Great Britain
by Amazon